# READING
# FARMERS' MARKET
## RECIPE BOOK

Published by MAP READING
on behalf of
Reading Farmers' Market

First published in 2002
© Reading Farmers' Market
Published by
MAP READING
20 Kidmore End Road
Emmer Green
Reading
Berkshire
RG4 8SE
**www.map-reading.co.uk**
No reproduction is permitted without
the prior permission of Reading Farmers' Market

ISBN 0-9534436-5-5

Recipes submitted by the stallholders of Reading Farmers' Market
Compilation and Editing by Margaret Ormonde
Photography by Clive Ormonde and others
Typesetting and design MAP READING
Printed by
Antony Rowe Ltd
Bumpers Farm
Chippenham
Wiltshire
SN14 6LH

Recipes originate from stallholders,
or a source that has given permission for their use.
It is believed that all recipes have been tested,
but individual conditions will vary and slight adjustments made
to suit individual need and tastes.

**Abbreviations used in this book are:**
tsp = teaspoon (5 ml)
dstsp = dessertspoon (10 ml)
tblsp = tablespoon (15 ml)

g = gram  oz = ounce
kg = kilogram  lb = pound
ml = millilitre  fl oz = fluid ounce
l = litre  pt = pint
cm = centimetre  in = inch

**Conversion tables:**
Weights and measures are given in metric and imperial.
Use **either one set or the other**, as they may not correspond exactly.
Assume unstated spoon measurements to be level and egg sizes to be medium.

| Weights | | Volume | | Dimensions | |
|---|---|---|---|---|---|
| 5 g | ¼ oz | 55 ml | 2 fl oz | 5 mm | ¼ inch |
| 10 g | ½ oz | 150 ml | 5 fl oz (¼ pt) | 1 cm | ½ inch |
| 25 g | 1 oz | 275 ml | 10 fl oz (½ pt) | 2.5 cm | 1 inch |
| 100 g | 4 oz | 425 ml | 15 fl oz (¾ pt) | 15 cm | 6 inches |
| 200 g | 8 oz | 570 ml | 1 pint | 20 cm | 8 inches |
| 400 g | 1 lb | 1.2 litres | 2 pints | 30 cm | 11½ inches |

**Oven Temperatures:**
Electric oven temperatures in recipes are given in degrees celcius.
Ovens should always be pre-heated.
Temperatures should be reduced for fan assisted ovens.

| Gas Mark | Electric | |
|---|---|---|
| ¼ | 120°C | 240°F |
| ½ | 130°C | 265°F |
| 1 | 140°C | 275°F |
| 2 | 150°C | 300°F |
| 3 | 170°C | 325°F |
| 4 | 180°C | 350°F |
| 5 | 190°C | 375°F |
| 6 | 200°C | 400°F |
| 7 | 220°C | 425°F |
| 8 | 230°C | 450°F |
| 9 | 240°C | 475°F |

**Microwave** cookery is not just for re-heating and in fact is ideal for any conventional cooking which requires water *(boiling, steaming, poaching)*. It is particularly good for cooking very fresh vegetables. The speedy cooking retains the natural moisture, preserves colour and texture and is therefore healthier. It is important that no salt is added until after cooking. It can soften chopped onions in seconds and cooks fruit in very little water, It is a good method for soups, sauces and steamed puddings, can soften butter, or melt chocolate. Microwave ovens are assumed to be 750 watt. Refer to your manufacturer's hand book.

# CONTENTS

Local Produce 6 - 7

The Market and the Stallholders 8 - 18

Fruit and Vegetables in Season 19 - 21

Recipes (22 - 87) :
1. Soups, Starters, Snacks
 and Vegetable Dishes 22 - 34
2. Salads 36 - 40
3. Poultry and Game 42 - 48
4. Meat 50 - 66
5. Fish 68 - 70
6. Puddings 72 - 80
7. Cakes 82 - 84
8. Miscellany 86 - 87

Suggested Menus 90 - 93

Index / Acknowlegements 94 - 96

# Local Produce

The prime purpose of this recipe book is to offer customers a wide variety of ideas and suggestions as to how they can make the best of Farmers' Market goods. The focus is on using fresh and wholesome produce and reintroducing the idea of eating 'in season' (see p19-20).

Although the book is devoted to Reading Farmers' Market, there are others in the Reading area who follow the same principles of promoting healthy eating, have an environmentally friendly outlook, and encourage the strengthening of the local economy and communities:

### True Food Club
**Tel:** (0118) 9546430
**Website:** http://roadbusters.members.gn.apc.org/truefood
**e-mail:** truefood@gn.apc.org
This is a non-profit group selling all-organic, local fresh foods and wholefoods. It meets twice a month and encourages members to bring surplus own-grown organic produce to meetings. Membership is free.

### Examples of retail outlets are:

### County Delicacies
35 St Mary's Butts, Reading
**Tel:** (0118) 9574653
Local products include cheeses from Village Maid in Riseley, Artisan Bakery bread from Abingdon, local honey from Caversham, ham on the bone from Beenham and 'biltong' (South African dried meat) from Reading.

### Frost's Fishmongers
11a Union Street, Reading
**Tel:** (0118) 9505393 / 9574627
Fresh fish on sale including local trout.

### Vicar's Butchers
20 West Street, Reading    **Tel:** (0118) 9572904
Local specialities include venison and game.

### The Fruit Shop at Wellers
Reading Road, Burgfield Common RG7 3BL **Tel:** (0118) 9835333 / 9833434
Produce includes free-range eggs and local honey.

There are other local outlets who also support the Farmers' Market and their details can be found in the relevant section - **Bloomfield Hatch Farm Shop** (p 15), **Boze Down Vineyard** (p 18), **Buckhold Hill Farm** (p12), **Cross Lanes Fruit Farm** (p 12), **Englefield Organic Growers** (p12), **Garlands Organic Shop** (p 13). **WI Markets** (p 16), are held regularly in Reading and the surrounding area.

## Fair Trade

Not everything can be grown locally. When buying food that can only be produced in hot countries, like many fruits, tea and coffee, then it is equally important to make sure that the local producers overseas reap the benefits of direct trade. 'Fairtrade' status is only awarded to products that meet a strict set of criteria, including: decent wages, minimum health and safety standards, a fair price, a long term trading commitment and good environmental standards. Reading is becoming a 'Fairtrade' town- look out for the logo on goods in both specialist shops and many local supermarkets.
For more information contact:

**Reading International Solidarity Centre** (RISC)
35-39 London Street, Reading RG1 4PS
**Tel:** (0118) 9586692  **Fax:** (0118) 9594357
**Website:** www.risc.org.uk
**e-mail:** risc@risc.org.uk

**Local Cafés supporting local producers and a 'Fairtrade' policy include:**

**Café Iguana**
11 St Mary's Butts, Reading RG1 2LN
**Tel:** (0118) 9581357 / 9597191
-vegetables from Englefield Organic Growers.

PHOTO, WENDY TOBITT

**Global Café**
35 London Street, Reading RG1 4PS  **Tel:** (0118) 9583555
'Fairtrade' enterprise (see RISC above), also using local produce, such as WI cakes, Englefield Organic Growers' vegetables, Park Farm organic meat and Frost's local trout.

## Reading Farmers' Market

At the core of the market are the local farmers. Meat and dairy produce is there continuously. Fruit and vegetable growers, either come on a seasonal basis or, try to vary the goods they have to offer throughout the year.

The market is enhanced by other local stallholders, who, although are not prime producers, do prepare their goods locally, often using FM produce. These include biscuit and cake makers, jams, pickles and sauces, fruit and alcoholic drinks. Also at the market are a number of of plant growers - **Stevenson Road Nursery**, Wantage, **APS Plants**, Reading, and **THRIVE** a local community group.

It is also assumed that the cook will have a basic **store cupboard** - flour, milk, milk products, fat or oil, seasoning, dried fruit, rice, sugar, lemon juice and for the occasional indulgence, chocolate. Many of the recipes advocate the use of fresh herbs. These can be grown from plants sold at the market. Store cupboard goods need not necessarily be confined to standard supermarkets (see section above on local producers and 'Fairtrade'). Watch out for a new milk product sold in aid of the Wildlife Trusts, called 'White and Wild' which will soon be readily available - www.whiteandwild.co.uk.

At the back of this book are suggested menus using recipes from the book. These also include ready-made accompaniments - wine, beer, breads, biscuits.

# READING FARMERS' MARKET

Contact Mark Hillyer Tel: 07904 521434, e-mail: readingfm@supanet.com

The first trial markets were organised in late 1999 by Reading Borough Council, as part of their promotion of sustainability. The current market meets between 9.00 am and 12.30 pm at the Cattle Market in Great Knollys Street, usually on the first and third Saturdays in the month. Shoppers can buy fresh, quality, locally produced food and meet the local farmers and growers. Stallholders offer fruit, vegetables, meat, poultry and fish, cheese and wines, fruit drinks, bread, cakes, pies and biscuits. The market is now an independent community enterprise, but supported by Reading Borough Council. It belongs to the Thames Valley Farmers' Market Association - www.thamesvalleyfarmersmarket.co.uk and is amember of the National Association of Farmers'Markets www.farmersmarkets.net Tel: (01225) 787914.

# Meat, Poultry and Fish

Clearwater, East Hendred,
near Wantage, Oxfordshire, OX12 8LN
**Tel / Fax:** (01235) 820500
**Website:** www.trouttrader.co.uk

Trout is farmed the whole year round in areas where there is pure, cool water in rivers and lakes. Brookleas Fish Farm, run by Tim Lobb, was established in 1979, on the beautiful site of an old mill on the East Hendred Brook at Ludbridge. The typical chalk stream on which it is based rises a few miles away on the downs and joins the River Thames at Abingdon. There is a shop at the farm and a 'catch your own' pool.

Quick and easy to cook, trout is a very fine convenience food and also one of the healthiest. Like other oily fish it contains significant quantities of Omega 3, thought to help prevent and control heart disease. It is low in calories as well as being a very useful source of vitamins A, B1, B2, C & D.

Brookleas attend the first Reading Farmers' Market in each month.

## Bucklebury Farm Park

Bucklebury, Reading, Berkshire RG7 6RR
**Tel:** (0118) 9714002
**Fax:** (0118) 9714151

Rupert Hartley-Russell began cattle and sheep farming in the 1980s, then established his deer herd in 1992. The deer, currently numbering 120, roam on part of 70 acres of parkland and it is believed there were deer on the site hundreds of years ago. The deer are of Scottish wild stock with additions of English Park and German bloodlines. There are also some Fallow deer in the herd.

The park is open for visitors daily from early spring to September, and at weekends and holidays throughout the year. Venison is on sale at Reading Farmers' Market on the first Saturday of each month.

## Callows Farm

The Ridings, Stonesfield, near Witney, Oxon OX8 8EG
**Tel:** (01869) 891172

David Holloway started farming in 1990 and has a small herd of outdoor pigs and a few sheep. The pigs are bred outside and finished in a stress-free, straw based system. They produce dry-cured bacon (green and smoked), five varieties of sausages, gammon and all fresh pigmeat joints. He also rears free-range hens for their eggs and some 250 free-range Bronze turkeys for the Christmas trade. David and his wife Selena attend every Reading Farmers' Market and eight others in the Thames Valley.

PHOTO, DEWS MEADOW FARM

## Dews Meadow Farm
Oxford Road, East Hanney, Wantage, Oxon OX12 0HP **Tel:** (01235) 868634
**e-mail:** dews_meadow_shop@yahoo.co.uk

Jane and Andy Bowler have been pig farmers since 1979, supplying traditional home produced pork and bacon to the public since 1986. The pigs are bred outside and finished in a straw-based, stress-free system. The award-winning dry cured bacon *(green and smoked)* is particularly popular. In the year 2000 they achieved the acolade of 'The World's Best Bacon Award'. They specialise in gluten free products. They attend seven Thames Valley Farmers' Markets and run their own shop.

## Foxbury Farm
Colin Dawes, Foxbury Farm, Burford Road, Brize Norton, Oxfordshire OX18 3NX
**Tel:** (01993) 844141 **e-mail:** colin@foxburyfarm.co.uk
**Website:** www.foxburyfarm.co.uk

The Dawes family, currently farming on the edge of the Cotswolds, have a long tradition of farming in the Reading / Henley area and using Reading Livestock Market to sell meat to local butchers. The growth of the supermarkets has had a dramatic effect on local butchers and livestock markets. Reading

PHOTO, FOXBURY FARM

Farmers' Market has enabled them to revisit old territory and sell direct to customers. Foxbury Farm covers 500 acres, with 700 breeding ewes, 70 suckle cows and all their young stock. All the beef and lamb is now sold through the Farm Shop and Farmers' Markets. By adopting a natural farming policy, all the lambs are born outside in April, where they remain, reared with their mothers on grass. This gives the meat a more mature and natural flavour.

## Ixhill Farm
Dennis & Barry Cox, Ixhill Farm, Oakley, Aylesbury, Buckinghamshire HP18 9FQ **Tel:** (01844) 338855

This is a family run business covering about 200 acres on the Bucks/Oxon border *(about a mile from the infamous Leatherslade Farm - secret hideout of the Great Train Robbers!)*. The farm has been in the family for over 100 years and has arable farmland, sheep and poultry. Ixhill Farm are at every Reading Farmers' Market.

PHOTO, IXHILL FARM

## Kiln Meadows Farm
Cox's Lane, Midgham, Reading, Berkshire RG7 5UR
**Tel:** (0118) 9712138

Gordon and Val Hedges have been farming Pedigree Highland Cattle at Midgham since 1980. They are not strictly organic, but have the welfare of the animals at heart and minimise the use of chemicals and sprays on their land. All foodstuffs are completely natural and the calves stay with their mothers until they are eight months old. Just before 30 months old they are sent to a local slaughterhouse. The mature, well flavoured meat is then hung on the bone for three weeks. A full range of Highland beef products is on sale at every Reading Farmers' Market throughout the year.

## Redways Farm
New Inn Road, Beckley, Oxford OX3 9US
**Tel:** (01865) 351331 **Fax:** (01865) 351991

Michael Eadle has kept pigs since starting in the back yard of his parents' home in the 1960s. He now runs two farms near Oxford, where all the pigs are kept outdoors. With butchery knowledge learnt from his army days, Michael is able to breed, rear and butcher his own pigs. Son Robert has joined the business which now sells a variety of products including low fat sausages, dry cured bacon, pies, and old time favourites like chitlings, brawn and Bath chaps.

## Riverwood Farm
New Mill Road, Finchampstead, Berkshire RG40 4QT
**Tel:** (0118) 9731702 **Website:** www.ostrich-meat.co.uk

The farm, run by the Hitti family, covers 15 acres of beautiful countryside. The ostriches range from 1 day old chicks to 7 year old breeders. They graze on the land and in addition are fed special dietary pellets. There is a farm shop and, as well as attending Reading Farmers' Market, they also trade at Newbury, Marlow, and Wokingham.

Ostrich meat is very versatile and has many excellent qualities. It is the healthiest 'red' meat available - low in fat, calories and cholesterol and high in iron, calcium and protein. The meat is available as fillet and prime steaks, diced steak for casseroles, stir-fry and burgers and sausages.

# Fruit and Vegetables

## Buckhold Hill Farm
Pangbourne, Reading, Berkshire RG8 8QE
**Tel:** (0118) 9744388

Rod and Robin Ward run this 'pick-your-own' soft fruit and vegetable farm, which in season is open from 9.00am - 6.00pm, seven days a week. Strawberries, gooseberries, raspberries, currants, peas, potatoes and broad beans are included in their range. The produce is available at the Farmers'' Market, and ready picked orders can also be made over the telephone and collected from the farm shop.

## Cross Lanes Fruit Farm
Mapledurham, Reading, Berkshire, RG4 7UW
**Tel:** ( 0118) 972 3167
**e-mail:** apples@crosslanesfruitfarm.co.uk
**Website:** www.crosslanesfruitfarm.co.uk

Cross Lanes Fruit Farm, run by Dennis and Gill Franklin is a small orchard and farm shop, only four miles from Reading, growing apples, plums and pears. The orchard was begun by a previous owner in the 1940s and a few of the original trees remain. The last decade has seen a comprehensive replanting programme, both to renew traditional varieties and add some exciting new ones to the collection, to ensure top quality and flavour. There are over sixty different varities ranging from some old English favourites like Blenheim Orange, Cox's Orange Pippin and Peasgood Nonsuch, to newcomers including crisp and juicy Katy and Gloster 69.

Over the season, which runs from late August until early January you can buy the fruit, freshly pressed juices and honey from either the farm shop, Wednesday - Sunday, 10 am - 6 pm, or at Reading and other local Farmers' Markets.

## Englefield Organic Growers
57 Radstock Road, Newtown, Reading, Berkshire RG1 3PS
**Tel:** (0118) 9260783 / 9745428

Jez Taylor, who runs the business, has been operating since 1998. The produce is grown at two sites, one on the Englefield Estate and the other at Folly Farm in Sulhampstead. They produce a wide range of salads and vegetables supplying Reading, Wallingford and Henley Farmers' Markets. They also run a local bag delivery scheme in the summer. They supply three local restaurants including The Global Café and Iguana Café in Reading. Englefield Organic Growers are fully certified with the Soil Association

Small-scale market gardening, growing a diverse range of produce, sold direct to the customer is a viable livelihood for any energetic, enthusiastic horticulturalist, especially in Berkshire where the demand is so high.

**Garlands ORGANIC**

6 Reading Road, Pangbourne,
Reading, Berkshire RG8 7LY
**Tel:** (0118) 9844770

Garlands Organic, run by Denise Ingrem and Gabriel Hutchings, is a specialist organic health food shop promoting a healthy and ecologically sound lifestyle. It was established in 1990 and makes regular appearances at the Reading Farmers' Market from the end of June to late October.

Seasonal vegetables were initially grown at Upper Basildon, but moved to a one hectare market garden near the A4 at Beenham in 1999, when the original garden became too small. Although vegetable production is continuous, winter crops are limited to salads and a few leeks and brassicas. The first sowings are tomatoes in January, and the main production period is summer and early autumn. Gabriel Hutchings manages the garden, assisted by a part-time person during the peak season.

## The Herb Garden

Kingston House Estate, Kingston Bagpuize Oxfordshire OX13 5AU
**Tel: / Fax:** (01865) 820159

Pete and Val Williams, who run this enterprise, offer a wide selection of culinary and medicinal herbs and dye plants together with over fifty varieties of lavender.

## Highclose Farm

Chilton House, Charnham Lane, Hungerford, Berkshire RG17 0SP
**Tel:** (01488) 686770

Highclose Farm, a family-owned business managed by Steve Gallimore, is committed to the sale of high quality fruit, vegetables and luxury food for the discerning customer. As well as attending regular Farmers' Markets they also run a 'pick-your-own' area of 40 acres of fruit and vegetables and a farm shop on the Bath Road midway between Hungerford and Marlborough. Another twenty acres of vegetables are grown at Thatcham, including ten acres of organic vegetables.

## Peter Mushrooms
Sandhill Farm, Picketts Hill, Sleaford, Near Bordon, Hampshire GU35 8TF
**Tel:**(01420) 478366 **Fax:** (01730) 892990

Rollo Rosetti has been involved in mushroom production since 1972 and in 1984 set up his own business on a greenfield site, growing mushrooms in bags in heated polytunnels. They are mainly flat mushrooms, but also include buttons, cups and chestnuts. The popularity of local farmers' markets has seen the production of specialist products using mushrooms and other fresh ingredients - soups, marinades, concentrates, ketchup and dried mushrooms. Peter Mushrooms attends every Reading market.

## Tilehurst Allotments Society
Jenny Cottee, 85 Westwood Road, Tilehurst, Reading, Berkshire RG31 5PY
**Tel:** (0118) 9425169

PHOTO, TILEHURST ALLOTMENTS SOCIETY

The 75 plot-holders rent land from the Tilehurst Poor Lands Charity. (*A recent application to build on part of the land has been fiercely resisted.*) The seasonal produce on offer at Reading Farmers' Market is surplus to the needs of their families and friends. Every plot is managed in a different way, but the common factor is that the produce is local, fresh and that pesticides are rarely used. Crops include beetroot, elephant garlic, celeriac and a range of greens. Cooking tips and advice to potential gardeners are given freely.

## Waltham Place Farm
Church Hill, White Waltham, near Maidenhead, Berkshire SL6 3JH
**Tel:** (01268) 829096 / 825517

As organic kitchen garden suppliers to the Waltham Place Estate, they also sell direct to the public including at farmers' markets. An education programme is being developed whereby the kitchen garden will be used as a resource for learning, with the gardeners doing some outreach work.

## Westfield Farm
Cholsey, Oxfordshire OX10 9LS  **Tel:** (01491) 651357

The Gibbons family have ben farming and selling potatoes direct to the public since 1964. The farm on the edge of the Berkshire Downs, includes an area of the ancient Thames flood plain, where the soil is black silt.The main farm crops are wheat for bread-making and barley for malt (beer). The potatoes are rotated on the black silty half of the farm. The 20 acres yield 300 tons of eating potatoes. The varieties - Obelix, Wilja, King Edwards - are chosen for their flavour and cooking quality. Since many small greengrocers have closed, due to fierce competition, the Farmers' Markets have provided the opportunity to again sell distinctive, flavoursome potatoes in local towns.

# Dairy Produce

## Abbeygold Cheese
6 Winter Lane, West Hanney, near Wantage, Oxfordshire OX12 0LF
**Tel:** (01235) 868705
**Website:** www.abbeygoldcheese.com   **e-mail:** abbeygold@aol.com

This award winning enterprise started in 1985 initially supplying the milk from a flock of dairy ewes to other cheese producers. Some was retained for sale to local health food shops and some for people with allergies to cheese and goats milk. Subsequently ewes' milk yoghurt was made and then a variety of different cheeses was developed. Traditional cheese making involves coagulating the milk with animal based rennet. Due to the demand for vegetarian products all Abbeygold cheeses are made with non-animal rennet. Cheeses include both hard and soft types. They attend most Reading Markets

## Bloomfield Hatch Farm
Mortimer, near Reading, Berkshire RG7 3AD
**Tel:** (0118 ) 9332540  **Fax:** (0118) 9332541

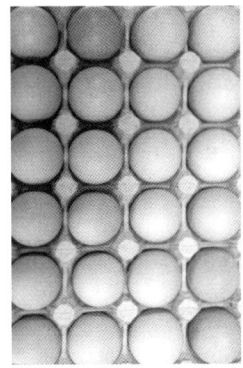

Steve and Joni Davies have been running the farm since 1984. Their main business is the production of free-range eggs. The chicken are fed on non GM ingredients, free from artificial colourings. They also have some sheep and cattle, and at Christmas time sell fresh turkeys. Other services they offer include tree surgery and the re-filling of summer hanging baskets. Bloomfield Hatch has won the 'Best Farmed Farm' award under 300 acres, in their local area. They attend every Reading Farmers' Market.

## Twineham Grange Farm
Bob Lane, Haywards Heath, Sussex RH17 5NH
**Tel:** (01444) 881394
**e-mail:** enquiries@twinehamgrangefarms.co.uk
**Website:** www.twinehamgrangefarms.co.uk

The company was established in 1975 and since 1985 has been producing high quality 100% natural, Italian style cheeses. It specialises in the production of 'Parmesan' cheese, which can take anything up to eighteen months to produce. The milk which comes from traditionally fed cows, is left to stand once it reaches the creamery, to allow the cream to rise naturally. Using traditional Italian equipment, the cheesemaker cooks each vat individually. After three days in a carefully controlled environment, the cheese is immersed in brine for 21 days and constantly inspected. Finally it is laid to rest in the cheese store until it reaches full maturity. They have recently introduced a range of other cheeses, such as Ricotta and Provolone, not currently available at Farmers' Markets. Check out the Twineham Grange website for full details and forthcoming attendances at local markets in the south-east. They usually sell at the second Reading Farmers' Market in the month.

# Bread, Cakes and Preserves

## Anila, Curry Sauces
37 Shaldon Way, Walton-on-Thames, Surrey KT12 3DJ
**Tel:** / **Fax:** (01932) 229095
**e-mail:** anilas_sauces@hotmail.com

Anila Vaghela began making sauces for family and friends over ten years ago. By 1997 she was able to launch her business supplying delis, farm shops and specialist food stores. The establishment of the Farmers' Markets offered yet another outlet. In the years 2000 and 2001 the business received the Great Taste Awards for the sauces. New varieties are being introduced all the time including a range of chutneys and pickles.

## Earley W I Market
Janette Rawlings, Controller
**Tel:** (0118) 961 7496   **e-mail:** js.rawlings@ntlworld.com

WI markets have been in existence for over eighty years and were set up to give local producers an outlet for their goods and to serve the local community with good quality home-made produce. Each Market is run as a co-operative and Earley specialises in a lot of baked goods and preserves using traditional recipes. All WI cooks are required to have a Food Hygiene Certificate. Many of the ingredients come from the Farmers' Market: free-range eggs by the hundred, for cakes; and fruit and vegetables for their range of preserves. They are happy to take special orders. Attend every market.

## Emmanuel Methodist Church
Mrs Ivy Newman, 100 Waverley Road, Reading, Berkshire RG30 2PY
**Tel:** (0118) 9583909

Mrs Newman specialises in jams and chutneys using organically grown fruit and vegetables from her own garden. She is continuing a longstanding family tradition, with her father a professional gardener and her mother a gifted cook. The preserves are for sale at Reading Farmers' Market on the first Saturday in each month. Profits go directly to Emmanuel Methodist Church, towards funding a new building.

## Home Farm
Heckfield, Hook, Hampshire RG27 0LP
**Tel:** (0118) 9326387   **e-mail:** c.a.harnett.son@fwi.co.uk

Home Farm is a 500 acre dairy and arable enterprise run by the Harnett family. Ninety percent of the ingredients in their jams are either picked from the farm hedgerows eg. blackberries and wild plums, grown in their garden eg. apples, plums and redcurrants, or purchased from a local pick-your-own enterprise. They began making jam and preserves for their own consumption and won prizes at local horticultural shows. The setting up of local Farmers' Markets gave them the opportunity to expand the business and they now attend every Reading Farmers' Market.

## Just Biscuits
5 Wykeham Way, Haddenham, Buckinghamshire HP17 8BL
**Tel:** (01844) 291350  **e-mail:** justbiscuits@hotmail.com

Sally Bent has been in the food industry throughout her working life, and, when local Farmers' Markets were established, spotted a niche for home-made, freshly baked biscuits in sweet and savoury flavours. These include a variety of shortbread and oat biscuits, the savoury ones using different cheeses. As well as being delicious in their own right, they make suitable accompaniments for some of the recipes in this book.

Sally attends Reading Farmers' Market at the beginning of each month as well as markets in Bicester, Henley, Thame and Maidenhead.

## Lintrithan Apiary
75 Branksome Hill Road, College Town,
Sandhurst, Berkshire GU47 0QF
**Tel: / Fax** (01276) 35545

The apiary, run by Jim Chambers has over 300 hives, producing honey in the counties of Berkshire, Hampshire, Oxfordshire, Wiltshire and Dorset. They provide, honey in jars and cut combs, honey marmalade, as well as some non-edible products - honey handcreams, beeswax candles, beeswax furniture cream and polish. Attend every Reading Farmers' Market.

## Olives
Jeremy Phillips, 'Buddleia', 1 St Annes Close, Winchester, Hampshire SO22 4LQ  **Tel: / Fax:** (01962) 870377

The olives themselves might come from Mediterranean climes - Morocco, Spain, Italy and Greece, but they are processed using marinades made from local ingredients, including mushrooms, sweet peppers and a variety of herbs.

## Vincent Charles
Great Farm Park Cottages, Mortimer, near Reading RG7 3AA
**Tel:** (0118) 9332 862  **e-mail:** vincentcharles75@hotmail.com

English Bakers of the Year, for two successsive years, Vince Charles began selling his award winning, high quality organic bread at Reading Farmers' Market in the year 2000. There are Italian specialities, 100% rye loaves, no added yeast loaves amongst many others. The bread is just part of a much wider catering enterprise suppling local quality organic goods for functions, conferences and local authorities.

17

# Beverages

**BENSONS** PURE ENGLISH APPLE JUICE

Stones Farm, Sherborne, Gloucestershire GL54 3HD
**Tel:** (01451) 844117
**e-mail:** bensons.applejuice@virgin.net
**Website:** www.bensonsapplejuice.co.uk

PHOTO, BENSONS

There are 8 different varieties of apple juice on offer, each bottle containing the juice of twelve apples. They contain no added sugar, colourings or preservatives and have a one year shelf life.

### Boze Down Vineyard
Hardwick Road, Whitchurch-on-Thames, Reading RG8 7QS
**Tel:** (0118) 9844031
**e-mail:** info@bozedown.com  **Website:** www.bozedown.com

Run by Richard Conn, the vineyard lies on 5 acres of chalk and flint soil at the southern end of The Chilterns, near the Thames. It was first planted in the mid-1980s and grows 4 red (*an English rarity*) and 5 white, medal winning, varieties of grapes. The wines are made by John Worontschak, an Australian flying winemaker, who enjoys the challenge of making world class wines in the fickle English climate. Chemicals are kept to the minimum, and fertilizer provided by winter grazing sheep. Boze Down Vineyard shop opens weekends March to December.

### The Chiltern Brewery
Nash Lee Road, Terrick,
Aylesbury, Buckinghamshire, HP17 0TQ
**Tel:** (01296) 613547  **Fax:** (01296) 612419
**Website:** www.chilternbrewery.co.uk

The ancient and revered art of the English brewer is alive and flourishing at The Chiltern Brewery, which was established by Richard and Lesley Jenkinson in 1980. Their brewery specialises in the production of hand-crafted draught and bottled beers. They also produce a unique range of goods made with beer, hops or malt, including prize-winning cheeses, bread, chocolate, hop pickled onions and hop cologne, all of which are available through the brewery shop. It also houses the fascinating Buckinghamshire Breweries Museum.

### Hunny Corner Cottage Plants /Traditional Farmhouse Drinks
Old Coach House, Wokingham Road, Bracknell, Berkshire RG42 1PP
**Tel:** (01344) 455160  **e-mail:** lesley@dialstart.net

Robin and Lesley Drinkwater grow organically produced herbs and other plants, including unusual perennials sourced from specialist nurseries. They also produce homemade drinks free of additives and artificial flavourings - wherever possible using their own fruits. The drinks include tayberry, blackberry, elderflower, damson, rhubarb, lemonade and two special winter warmers - hot ginger punch and hot orange with caramel.

# Fruit and Vegetables in Season

Surprisingly the concept of eating food in season does offer variety and scope. Many vegetables store well - onions and root vegetables, and others can be prepared for freezing. Some have a very short season and shelf life, giving us something to look forward to and savour - the smell and taste of English strawberries, the flavour of the first new potato, recently dug from the soil, flavoursome tomatoes..................

The following is a guide to seasonal availibility. Cooking times depend on the type of vegetable. Brassicas *(cabbage family)* are best under-cooked to preserve flavour and nourishment. Legumes *(peas and beans)* need little more than 10 minutes. Root vegetables need the longest cooking time. Salads should be freshly prepared to be at their best.

## All year round:
Beetroot
Carrots
Garlic
Mushrooms
Onions
Pototoes
Turnips
Watercress

## Spring:
Asparagus
Broccoli
Cabbage

## Spring / Summer:
Radishes
Rhubarb
Spring Onions

**Summer:**
Artichokes
Aubergine
Broad Beans
Cabbage
Corn-on-the-cob
Courgettes
Cucumber
French Beans
Gooseberries
Peas
Raspberries
Red / Blackcurrants
Strawberries

**Summer / Autumn:**
Apples
Blackberries
Cherries
Endive
Lettuce
Pears
Peppers, Green or Red
Plums
Runner Beans
Spinach
Tomatoes

**Summer / Autumn / Winter:**
Cauliflower
Marrow

**Autumn / Winter:**
Brussel Sprouts
Celeriac
Celery
Chicory
Horseradish
Pumpkin
Squash
Red Cabbage
Shallots
Swedes
Sweet Potatoes

**Winter / Spring:**
Cabbage
Curly Kale
Leeks
Parsnips

20

# SOUPS, SNACKS, STARTERS & VEGETABLE DISHES

# Cream of Mushroom Soup

**Ingredients**
200 g / ½ lb mushrooms, peeled and chopped
1 small onion, skinned and sliced
1.2 litres / 2 pints white stock
½ blade of mace
salt and freshly ground pepper
25 g / 1 oz flour
2 tblsp single cream
1 egg yolk

**Method**
   Put the prepared mushrooms, onions and stock into a saucepan. Bring them to the boil and simmer for 30 minutes. Liquidise.
   Melt the butter in a saucepan, add the flour and cook for a few minutes, stirring continuously. Slowly add the mushroom mixture and bring to the boil stirring until the mixture thickens. Season to taste.
   Mix the egg yolk and the cream together and add to them a cupful of the hot soup. Mix this with the rest of the soup, reheat, but do not boil.

# Pea and Ham Soup with Croûtons

**Ingredients**
200 g / ½ lb shelled peas
1 medium onion, chopped
1 small lettuce, sliced
50 g / 2 oz butter
425 ml / ¾ pt gammon stock (see p64)
425 ml / ¾ pt water
½ tsp sugar
freshly ground pepper
3 tblsp cream
2 thick slices of white bread, buttered on both sides and diced

**Method**
   Prepare the croûtons by toasting the diced bread in the oven until crisp and golden.
   Melt the butter and add the peas, lettuce and onion. Cover the pan and cook very slowly for about 25 minutes, until the vegetables are tender. Cool slightly, then blend in the liquidiser. Return to the pan and add the stock, water, sugar and seasoning. Simmer for about ten minutes. Remove from the heat to mix in the cream. Pour into bowls and sprinkle with the croûtons.

# Apple Vichyssoise *(Cold Apple Soup)*

## Ingredients
6 dessert apples *(preferably ripe Cox's Orange Pippin)* peeled, cored and chopped
2 potatoes, peeled and diced
1 small onion, peeled and finely chopped
1 clove of garlic, crushed
1 tsp curry powder
½ tsp salt, if liked
425 ml / ¾ pt stock *(chicken or vegetable, mild in flavour)*
150 ml / ¼ pt milk
150 ml / ¼ pt cream
chives or thin apple slices for garnish

## Method
Put the apples, potatoes, onion, garlic and salt into a large saucepan and cover with the stock. Bring to the boil and cook for half an hour, until soft. Mix the milk, cream and curry powder. Put some of the cooked apple mixture and some of the milk mixture into a liquidiser and blend until smooth, then pour into a bowl, repeating until all is used. Stir and check the seasoning. Chill for 2 hours. Serve, garnishing with the chives or thin apple slices.

PHOTO , CROSS LANES FRUIT FARM

# Potato and Leek Soup

## Ingredients
3 large leeks
1 large onion, sliced
400 g/ 1lb potatoes
60 g / 2½ oz butter
570 ml / 1 pt chicken or vegetable stock
150 ml / ¼ pt cream
chopped chives

## Method
Peel and slice the potatoes thinly. Wash the leeks thoroughly and slice thinly. Melt the butter in a heavy saucepan and add the leeks, potatoes and onion. Cover and cook very slowly over a low heat for 20 - 30 minutes, stirring occasionally. Add the stock and seasoning. Bring to the boil, cover and simmer for about 40 minutes until the vegetables are soft. Cool slightly and purée in a liquidiser. Return to the saucepan. Check the seasoning again and reheat, but do not boil. Remove from the heat, cool slightly and stir in the cream. Sprinkle with the chopped chives.

## Carrot and Butternut Squash Soup
*This recipe can be used with any of the squash family, even pumpkins*

**Ingredients**
2 tblsp olive oil
1 large onion, peeled and chopped
1 celery stalk, sliced
4 - 6 tomatoes, fresh or tinned
1 tsp ground coriander
½ tsp ground cumin
pinch of cinnamon
200 g / 8 oz carrots, peeled and chopped
1 butternut squash, peeled and chopped
1.8 litres / 3 pints vegetable stock
salt and freshly ground pepper

**Method**
    Heat the oil in the saucepan and fry the onions slowly for 5 -10 minutes. Add the celery, carrots and squash and cook slowly for a further 10 minutes. Stir in the spices; mix well together and cook for a few minutes more before adding the tomatoes and the stock. Simmer until soft, then liquidise in a blender *(can be sieved for special occasions)*. Reheat to serve, adding more stock if required. Check the seasoning and add fresh chopped parsley or coriander if available.

## Carrot and Orange Soup

**Ingredients**
400 g / 1 lb carrots, peeled and sliced
1 small onion, skinned and chopped
3 strips of orange peel *(use a potato peeler)*
salt and freshly ground pepper
25 g / 1 oz butter
720 ml / 1¼ pts chicken stock
1 bay leaf
a little cream or natural yoghurt

**Method**
    Melt the butter in a large saucepan, add the vegetables and cook for ten minutes. Pour on the stock and add the strips of orange, the bay leaf and seasoning. Bring to the boil, cover and simmer for 15 minutes. Remove the bay leaf, and liquidise the soup in a blender. Taste and adjust seasoning as necessary. Serve with a swirl of cream or natural yoghurt.

# Thick Autumn Soup

*Cavolo Nero or Nero di Toscano are black robust kales. Chard, green kale or, at a push Savoy cabbage are suitable alternatives.*
*Serves 5 or 6*

## Ingredients
1 Cavolo Nero kale
2 medium onions, skinned and chopped
6 or 7 stalks of celery, chopped
200 g / 8 oz carrots,of scrubbed and chopped
100 g / 4 oz parsley, chopped
100 - 150 g / 4 - 6 oz of cooked cannelloni beans
2 or 3 cloves of garlic, crushed
1 can of tomatoes (400g)
200 ml / ¼ pt vegetable stock
extra virgin olive oil
freshly ground black pepper
one stale Ciabatta bread loaf

## Method
Put the garlic, onions, celery, carrot, and 75 % of the parsley in a large pan and fry slowly for about 15 minutes in 2 or 3 tblsp of olive oil. Cover the pan to keep in the flavours and stir occasionally to stop sticking. Pour in the tomatoes cover and cook for a further 10 minutes.

Chop up the Cavolo Nero - remove the stalks and cut them into pieces about 1 cm / ½ in long, then chop the leaves into quite large bits *(they all cook in about the same time)*. Add the kale to the rest of the vegetables and enough stock to cover mixture if necessary. Add half the beans. Cover and cook gently for 20 - 30 minutes.

Liquidise the rest of the beans and add to the soup. The soup should be thick. Add a generous helping of extra virgin olive oil, the rest of the chopped parsley and some freshly ground black pepper. Chunks of stale Ciabatta may be stirred in before serving.

## Curried Eggs

### Ingredients
6 free-range eggs
1 bottle of Anila's Mild Curry Sauce
a little water
fresh coriander

### Method
Hard boil the eggs and cut into halves or quarters. Arrange in a pan and pour over the sauce. Cook for 5 minutes. Add more water if required and simmer gently to re-heat. Serve garnished with the fresh coriander and serve with naan bread or chapatties.

## Devilled Eggs

### Ingredients
6 free-range eggs
3 tblsp mayonnaise (see p 36)
1 tblsp Chiltern Ale Mustard
paprika

### Method
Hard boil the eggs and cut in half lengthwise. Remove the yolks and place in a bowl. Add the mayonnaise and the mustard and mix together. Refill the egg white hole with the mixture and decorate with a sprinkling of paprika.
Serve with salad and brown bread.

## Stuffed Mushrooms

### Ingredients
1 x 15 cm / 4 in or 2 x 10 cm / 2½ in flat mushrooms
1 thick slice of brown bread, crumbled
grated lemon rind
fresh herbs - parsley, marjoram, thyme, chopped
salt and freshly ground pepper
1 free-range egg, beaten

### Method
Wipe the mushrooms, remove the stalks and lay the mushrooms cap down in a lightly oiled baking dish. Chop the stalks and add with the lemon rind, herbs and seasoning into the breadcrumbs. Bind the mixture with the egg and spread on top of the mushrooms. Bake for 20 minutes on 180°C or gas mark 4 until golden.

## Surprise Pears

*Delicious either as a starter or use a whole pear each for a tasty snack*

### Ingredients
2 ripe pears (Conference, Concorde or Glou Morceau)
100 g / 4 oz cottage cheese
50g / 2 oz salami, chopped
chives, chopped
lemon juice

### Method
Halve the pears and remove cores, then brush with lemon juice to prevent browning. Mix the cheese and salami and pile a quarter of the mixture on to each pear half. Garnish with the chives.

## Celery with Cheese Filling

### Ingredients
150 g / 6 oz Gorgonzola cheese
200 g / 8 oz Mascapone cheese
100 g / 4 oz walnut kernels
celery sticks
parsley

### Method
Cut both the cheeses into small pieces. Mix together with a fork to creamy consistency. Crumble the walnuts and add to the cheese. Remove the leaves from the celery and wash thoroughly. Cut the celery into 10 cm / 2½ in pieces and fill with the cheese mixture. Arrange on a plate and garnish with the parsley.

PHOTOS, TWINEHAM GRANGE

## Fried Mozzarella

### Ingredients
1 Mozzarella cheese
white flour for coating
2 free-range eggs
75 g / 3 oz fresh breadcrumbs
oil for frying

### Method
Cut the Mozzarella into thick slices and coat with the flour. Beat the eggs in a bowl and dip the floured slices into the eggs. Coat these slices in the breadcrumbs then fry in very hot oil. Dry them on a piece of kitchen paper and serve hot, with salad & warm crusty bread.

27

# Ravioli with Ricotta Filling

**Ingredients**
Pasta:
  300 g / 12 oz strong white flour
  2 free-range eggs
  1 tblsp olive oil
  pinch of salt
Filling:
  250 g / 10 oz Ricotta cheese
  3 tblsp breadcrumbs
  2 free-range eggs
  125 g / 5 oz boiled and minced spinach
  salt and pepper
Dressing:
  50 g / 2oz butter
  fresh sage leaves
  grated 'English style' Parmesan cheese

**Method**
    First, prepare the filling by mixing all the listed ingredients in a bowl. Then prepare the pasta dough, kneading all the ingredients together and working well until the dough is smooth. Using a rolling pin and board, or pasta machine, stretch thin layers of pasta. Place the filling in small quantities on to the pasta at small intervals. Cover this strip of pasta with another layer of pasta and pressing the edges together, cut into squares with a pasta cutter.
    Put a generous amount of water into a pan. Bring to the boil, add salt and cook the ravioli until they gently rise to the surface. Strain them, sprinkle with grated Parmesan and pour melted butter with fried sage over the top.

# Tomatoes with Parmesan and Ricotta Filling

**Ingredients**
6 large tomatoes
100 g / 4 oz 'English style' Parmesan cheese, grated
200 g / 8 oz Ricotta cheese
4 tsp olive oil
garlic
fresh herbs - parsley, basil, oregano, chopped
salt and freshly ground pepper
basil for garnish

**Method**
    Remove the tops of the tomatoes and take out the pulp and the seeds. Sprinkle with salt and leave upside down to dry.
    Blend together the Ricotta, Parmesan, salt and pepper, olive oil and add the ground garlic and chopped fresh herbs. Fill the tomatoes with this mixture and lay them on an oven tray. Bake for 20 minutes at 180°C gas mark 4.
    Garnish with fresh basil.

# Spinach, Leek and Cheese, with Pasta

**Ingredients**
200 g / 8 oz penne pasta
600 g / 1½ lb leeks
400 g / I lb spinach
100 g / 4 oz hard ewes' cheese (or standard Cheddar cheese), grated
4 - 5 tomatoes sliced
salt and freshly ground pepper
parsley
Sauce:
  50 g / I oz butter
  25 g / 1 oz plain flour
  425 ml / ¾ pt milk
  2 tblsp wholegrain mustard

**Method**
   Cook the pasta in water, according to the instructions on the packet and drain. Wash the leeks thoroughly and slice into chunks. Heat the oil in a large saucepan and cook the leeks for 4 - 5 minutes. Add the spinach and cook until the liquid has evaporated. Season with the salt and pepper.
   Make the sauce by melting the butter and blending in the flour to make a roux. Gradually add the milk and continue stirring to create a smooth consistency. Stir in the mustard and cook for a further 3 - 4 minutes.
   Oil a large ovenproof dish. Cover the bottom with layer of pasta, followed by half the vegetables and half the cheese. Add another layer of pasta and spoon over half of the sauce. Repeat layers finishing with the sauce. Place the tomatoes on the top and bake in the oven for 20 minutes at 190°C or gas mark 5. Decorate with the parsley.

PHOTO, TILEHURST ALLOTMENTS

# Vegetable Parcels

### Ingredients
25 g / 1 oz butter, melted
55 ml / 2 fl oz olive oil
12 -16 sheets filo pastry *(fully defrosted)*
100 g / 4 oz soft mild ewe's cheese
50 g / 2 oz French beans, topped and tailed
50 g /2 oz broccoli, cut into florets
1 small aubergine, cut into strips
1 courgette, cut into strips
50 g / 2 oz mushrooms, sliced
salt and freshly ground pepper
a little olive oil

### Method
　Bring a pan of water to the boil and blanch the vegetables for 30 seconds before plunging them into very cold water - as well as cooling them this will preserve the colour. Sauté the mushrooms in the oil until tender and mix with the blanched vegetables. Using one sheet of pastry at a time, brush each with the melted butter and oil mixture. Fold the pastry sheet in half to make a long strip. Put a piece of ewe's cheese and some of the cooked vegetable mixture at the end nearest you. Fold the pastry over the cheese to make a triangular shape. Continue folding, retaining the triangular shape until the pastry is used up. Repeat the process until all the parcels are made.
　Place on a lightly oiled baking tray and brush with melted butter at 190°C or gas mark 5 for 15 - 20 minutes. Transfer to a wire cooling rack. Serve warm with a tomato and basil salad *(see p39)*.

# Tofu and Coriander Cakes

### Ingredients
2 shallots, finely chopped
clove of garlic, crushed
200 g / 8 oz smoked tofu, mashed
100 - 150 g / 4 - 6 oz fresh breadcrumbs
100 g / 4 oz ground almonds
150 g / 6 oz carrot, grated
2 tablespoons fresh coriander, chopped.
2 free-range eggs
1 tblsp Shoyu *(soy sauce)*
olive oil

### Method
　Mix all the ingredients in a large bowl, divide into six equal portions, then shape into flat cakes. If the mix is too dry add a little olive oil. Fry slowly on each side for about 7 minutes or until crisp. Serve with sliced tomatoes and a mixed salad.

## Mash Stir-fry
*Serves 2 - 3*

### Ingredients
400 g / 1 lb potatoes *(approx)*
olive oil, seasoning and a little hot milk
1 medium onion, peeled and chopped
1 clove garlic, crushed
1 tsp peeled and grated root ginger *(optional)*
2 - 3 carrots, peeled and sliced in thin strips
handful of mange tout peas, trimmed
1 red pepper, sliced in strips
1 courgette, sliced
3 - 4 broccoli florets
2 - 3 tblsp sweetcorn, off the cob if available
100 g / 4 oz mushroom sliced
2 tblsp soy sauce
bacon / sausage *(optional)*

### Method
Peel, boil and mash the potatoes with a little oil, seasoning and the milk. Keep hot.

Stir fry the onion and garlic in oil. Gradually add the remainder of the vegetables, starting with the carrots and the sweetcorn and ending with the mushrooms; stir-fry until just done. Add the soy sauce and cook for one minute more. Fry the bacon and sausage, if required, and cut into chunks.

Pile the potatoes on to a plate and top with the stir-fried vegetables *(bacon and sausage)* and the juices.

## Celeriac and Potato Crunchy Mash
*Serves 5 - 6 as a side dish*

### Ingredients
400 g / 1 lb celeriac
600 g / 1½ lb potatoes
2 or 3 tablespoons hemp seeds
3 tblsp grated fresh 'English style' Parmesan cheese
2 tblsp fresh parsley, chopped
olive oil
2 tblsp black olives *(kalamata are best)*, stoned and cut in half
freshly ground black pepper

### Method
Scrub the potatoes and peel the celeriac. Cut into pieces - the celeriac should be in chunks about three times as large as the potatoes because it cooks more quickly. Put both vegetables together in a pan of unsalted water and cover. Bring to the boil and simmer until soft.

Drain. Add the hemp seeds and Parmesan cheese and a few grinds of black pepper, then mash together with some olive oil. Stir in the olives. Finally, mix in the parsley, then serve in a pre-heated dish. For a crispy top, sprinkle some Parmesan on top and place the dish under a hot grill for a few minutes.

## King Edward's Champ

**Ingredients**
900 g / 2 lb of King Edward potatoes
3 - 4 spring onions, chopped into small pieces
knob of butter
salt

**Method**
    Peel the potatoes and cut into even size chunks. Sprinkle with a little salt, steam until soft - approximately 20 -25 minutes.
    When the potatoes are cooked, remove from steamer and drain. Return to the saucepan and cover with a clean tea towel to soak up steam. Mash the potatoes with the knob of butter, mix in the chopped spring onion. Serve.

## Wilja Parsnip and Onion Roast

**Ingredients**
900 g / 2 lb of Wilja potatoes
900 g / 2 lb of parsnips
400 g / 1 lb of onions
olive oil for frying
freshly ground black pepper

**Method**
    Peel the potatoes and the parsnips, cut into even sized chunks and part boil or steam. Peel the onions and chop roughly. Using a large frying pan or wok, fry the onions in a little olive oil until silver. Drain the potatoes and parsnips stand for a couple of minutes. Add the potatoes and the parsnips to onions in pan, turning in the oil. Transfer to a baking tray and sprinkle with salt and freshly ground black pepper. Put into a pre-heated oven to roast at 200°C or gas mark 6, for about 1 hour.

## Roasted Parsnips with Honey and Mustard Glaze

**Ingredients**
900 g / 2 lb parsnips, cleaned and trimmed
2 tblsp vegetable oil
2 tblsp clear English honey
1 tblsp prepared mustard
½ tsp caraway seeds
salt and freshly ground pepper

**Method**
    Pre-heat the oven to 240°C or gas mark 9 . Halve the parsnips and cut into even sized pieces. Parboil for 5 minutes and drain off the liquid. Heat the oil in the roasting tin until it sizzles. Place the parsnips into the pan, season and roast for 25 minutes.
    Mix the honey, mustard and caraway seeds and brush this glaze over the parsnips. Roast for a further 10 minutes. Serve.

# Baked Sliced Potatoes

## Ingredients
900 g / 2 lb Wilja potatoes
butter or olive oil
1 garlic clove
1 small onion, sliced
2 rashers of bacon, diced *(optional)*
fresh herbs, chopped
salt and freshly ground pepper

## Method
    Grease an ovenproof dish with butter or brush with olive oil. Rub the greased dish with a clove of garlic. Scrub clean the potatoes and slice into even pieces, approximately 3 mm / eighth of an inch thick. Fry the onions and the bacon. Spread the first layer of potatoes in the dish. Dot with butter or oil and season. Top with the onions, bacon and a few chopped herbs. Continue to alternate the layers until all the ingredients are used up, finishing with a layer of potatoes. Brush the top layer with a little butter or oil.
    Cook in a pre-heated oven at 180°C or gas mark 4 for 1 hour until the potatoes are soft and browned. Alternatively, cook in a microwave on high for 10 minutes, then brush the top with butter or oil and brown in a hot oven for 10 - 20 minutes.

# Obelix Cheese and Bacon Jackets

## Ingredients
2 large Obelix potatoes
2 rashers of streaky bacon
75 g / 3 oz Cheddar cheese
knob of butter
salt and freshly ground black pepper

## Method
    Scrub two large Obelix potatoes, dry them, then prick them a few times with a fork. Cook in a pre-heated hot oven 190°C or gas mark 5, for 1¾ - 2 hours until the skins are crisp. Grill the bacon and chop it into small pieces. Grate the cheese. Remove the potatoes from the oven, then slit lengthways.
    When they are cool enough to handle, scoop out the centre of the potatoes keeping the skins whole, to refill, and place in large bowl. Mash the potatoes with a little butter, add salt and freshly ground black pepper to taste. Mix in the chopped bacon and 50 g / 2 oz of the cheese. Refill the potato skins with the above mixture and push down with the back of a spoon. Place the remaining cheese on top and return to the oven for 10 -15 minutes.
    Serve with a mixed salad.

## Broad Bean Special

**Ingredients**
400 g / 1 lb broad beans, shelled
1 small onion, skinned and sliced
1 clove of garlic, crushed
2 rashers of bacon, chopped
knob of butter
½ glass of white wine
salt and freshly ground pepper

**Method**
   Fry the onions, garlic and bacon bits in the butter before adding the broad beans. Pour in the white wine, season, cover and allow to simmer for about 5 minutes.

## Potato Samosas

*Makes 16 samosas*

**Ingredients**
Filling:
   400 g / 1 lb potatoes (*Obelix or Desirée*)
   ½ tsp whole cumin seeds
   ½ tsp whole black mustard seeds
   1 large onion, chopped
   100 g / 4 oz peas
   1 tsp salt
   ½ tsp chilli powder
   1 tsp garam masala
   ½ tsp tumeric powder
   1 tblsp lemon juice

Pastry:
   200 g / 8 oz plain flour
   125 ml / 4 fl oz water
   1 tblsp lemon juice
   pinch of salt
Paste:
   25 g / 1 oz plain flour
   100 ml / 3 fl oz water
oil for frying

**Method**
   Wash and peel the potatoes and boil for 10 minutes. Cut into small cubes. Heat a little oil in a frying pan. Fry the chopped onion, cumin and mustard seeds until golden brown. Add the potatoes, peas, spices, mix together well and cook for 2 minutes. Remove from the heat.
   Prepare the pastry by mixing all the ingredients into a soft dough. Divide into eight parts and shape into a ball. Sprinkle a little flour onto a work surface and roll each ball out flat into a circle about 17.5 cm / 7 ins diameter. Put a little oil into a frying pan and cook each one for 4 seconds on each side. Cut each one in half.
   Mix the flour and water to make a paste. Take the pastries and form into a cone, by joining the two corners together, then joining the straight sides together with the paste. Fill each of the cones with 2 - 3 tblsps of the potato mixture. Paste together round the edge of the cone to seal the samosa*.
   Deep fry the samosas in cooking oil until crispy.
*\* At this stage the samosas can be frozen for up to 6 weeks. Defrost 1 hour before cooking.*

# SALADS

# Salad Dressings

*High quality mayonnaise can be bought commercially, but, for those who prefer to make their own using free range eggs from the Farmers' Market, a recipe is included.*

## Mayonnaise

### Ingredients
2 large egg yolks
1 tsp dry mustard powder
1 tsp salt
½ tsp freshly ground pepper
275 ml / ½ pt olive oil
2 tblsp white wine vinegar

### Method
Put the egg yolks and seasonings in a large bowl. Mix thoroughly. Put the oil into a jug and add one drop to the eggs. Whisk. Add another drop and whisk again. When, and only when, the mixture begins to thicken the procedure can be speeded up and the oil poured in larger drops and finally in a steady trickle. Whisking should be continued throughout. If the mixture curdles it is because the oil has been added too fast. *(It can be rescued by starting with another egg yolk and adding the curdled sauce very gradually, in the same way as the oil was added to the original egg mixture.)* Finally, when all the oil has been added, slowly mix in the vinegar and stir well.

Adjust the seasoning to taste. Store in the refrigerator in a screw top jar, for up to a week.

## Honey Dressing

### Ingredients
3 tblsp clear English honey
6 tblsp lemon juice
1 tsp dry English mustard powder
1 tsp paprika
salt and freshly ground pepper
2 tblsp fresh parsley, chopped

### Method
Put all the ingredients into a bowl and blend together until smooth. Finally stir in the chopped parsley. Cover and refrigerate until ready to use over the salad *(which needs to be the same day)*.

# Italian Salad

**Ingredients**
200 g / 8 oz long grain rice
1 yellow pepper, cored, seeded and thinly sliced
1 red pepper, cored, seeded and thinly sliced
1 small can of beans, drained
½ a cucumber, peeled and diced
10 green olives, stoned and chopped
2 spring onions, chopped
Dressing:
  6 tblsp olive oil
  6 tblsp white wine vinegar
  1 tblsp fresh chopped basil
  1 garlic clove, crushed
  salt and freshly ground pepper

**Method**
Cook the rice in boiling salted water until it is tender. Strain and run under cold water to cool. When it has dried off, stir in the vegetables and mix well. Put the ingredients for the dressing into a screw top jar and shake well. Pour over the rice and vegetable mixture and stir well. Chill before serving.

# Winter Vegetable Salad

**Ingredients**
400g / 1 lb waxy potatoes *(eg Obelix or Desirée)*
1 large celery stalk, finely chopped
2 carrots, peeled and grated
1 red eating apple *(eg Spartan or Malling Kent)*, cored and chopped
½ a small white cabbage, core removed and finely shredded
10 black olives, stoned and chopped
4 tblsp mayonnaise *(see previous page for details)*
salt and freshly ground pepper

**Method**
Peel and cook the potatoes in salted water. Do not over cook. Drain them and leave to cool. Dice. Mix the diced potatoes with the chopped celery, carrots, apple, cabbage and olives.
Spoon on the mayonnaise and stir well. Season to taste.

# Potato and Egg Salad with Avocado Dressing

**Ingredients**
900 g / 2 lb baby new potatoes
2 tblsp chopped parsley
6 free-range eggs, hard boiled and quartered
1 onion thinly sliced
Dressing:
   1 avocado pear
   1 clove garlic, crushed
   1 tblsp lemon juice
   100 g / 4 oz sour cream or natural yoghurt
   2 drops of Tabasco sauce
   1 tsp clear English honey

**Method**
   Boil the potatoes until just tender. Drain and refresh under cold water. Place the cooked potatoes, parsley, eggs and onion in a large salad bowl and mix together. To make the dressing, place the garlic, lemon juice, sour cream or yoghurt, tabasco sauce and honey in a food processor or blender. At the last moment, peel and chop the avocado pear and add to the other ingredients. Blend until smooth.
   Just prior to serving, spoon the dressing over the salad.

# Marais Salad

**Ingredients**
1 small crisp lettuce, shredded
150 g / 6oz shelled peas, uncooked
6 hard-boiled eggs, chopped
100 g / 4 oz mushrooms, chopped
50 g / 2 oz grated Cheddar cheese
Topping:
   275 ml / 10 fl oz / ½ pt sour cream
   275 ml /10 fl oz / ½ pt mayonnaise
   4 tsp dry English mustard powder
   4 tsp lemon juice
   chopped crispy bacon or paprika

**Method**
   Layer the salad ingredients in a clear glass bowl. Begin with the lettuce, followed by the peas, eggs, mushrooms and cheese.
   Mix thoroughly together the cream, mayonnaise, mustard and lemon juice and spoon on top of the layered salad. Sprinkle with the crispy bacon or paprika.

# Tomato and Basil Salad

**Ingredients**
6 tomatoes, skinned and quartered
50 g / 2 oz black olives, pitted and sliced
25 g / 1 oz sun-dried tomatoes, drained and thinly sliced
1 red onion, skinned and thinly sliced
fresh basil to garnish
Vinaigrette:
    4 tblsp chopped fresh basil
    1 clove of garlic, crushed
    2 tblsp freshly grated 'English style' Parmesan cheese
    4 tblsp olive oil
    2 tblsp lemon juice
    freshly ground black pepper

**Method**
    Arrange all the prepared ingredients for the salad into a large bowl and mix together. In a small bowl put the ingredients for the vinaigrette and whisk together until well blended. Pour over the salad and garnish with the basil.

***Tip!***
*To skin a tomato, plunge into boiling water for one minute. Drain, then plunge immediately into cold water and the skin will split, ready for peeling.*

# Rocket and Strawberry Salad

**Ingredients**
1 large bag rocket leaves
400 g / 1 lb strawberries
olive oil to taste
balsamic vinegar to taste
salt and freshly ground pepper

**Method**
    Slice the strawberries and place in a salad bowl with the rocket leaves. Reserve some of the strawberries to put on the top to garnish the salad. Drizzle the olive oil and the balsamic vinegar, in roughly equal quantities, over the salad. Season with salt and pepper – toss, garnish with the reserved strawberries and serve.

***Fruity Tip!***
*Try serving raspberries in salad of endive. Dress with a little oil and raspberry vinegar and top with shavings of strong Cheddar or Parmesan cheese.*

# Trout and Mushroom Salad

**Ingredients**
400 g / 1lb smoked trout fillet, broken into large lumps
250 g / 10 oz thinly sliced button mushrooms

Vinaigrette :
  1 tblsp vinegar
  2 tblsp olive oil
  ½ tsp each, salt, pepper, sugar, mustard powder
lettuce
parsley, chopped

**Method**
   Toss the raw mushrooms in the vinaigrette and mix with the smoked trout. Serve on a bed of lettuce and garnish with the chopped parsley. Serve with brown bread and butter.

## Pasta and Cheese Salad

**Ingredients**
600 g / 1½ lb fresh pasta *(penne, fusilli, conchiglie)*
250 g / 10 oz Mozzarella cheese, cubed
4 tomatoes, skinned and chopped
100 g / 4 oz black olives, sliced thinly
fresh herbs - basil, oregano, chopped
4 tblsp olive oil
salt and freshly ground pepper

**Method**
   First, boil the pasta in a large pan of sufficient salted water until soft. Strain it under cold running water to prevent it from over cooking.
   In a bowl prepare the dressing, made of diced Mozzarella cubes, tomatoes and olives. Mix in the herbs, cooked pasta, olive oil and seasoning. Serve at room temperature.

## Smokey Crispy Bacon Salad

**Ingredients**
200 g / 8 oz dry cured smoked bacon
crisp lettuce, washed and sliced
1 red pepper, sliced
4 spring onions, sliced
¼ cucumber, chopped
2 sticks of celery, chopped
2 tblsp olive oil
1 tblsp white wine vinegar
salt and freshly ground pepper

**Method**
   Fry or grill the bacon until crisp and leave to get cold. Arrange the lettuce in a bowl and mix in with it all the other salad ingredients. Break up the bacon into pieces and sprinkle over the salad.
   Make a salad dressing by mixing well together the oil, vinegar and seasoning. Drizzle over the salad.

# POULTRY & GAME

chicken
pigeon
rabbit
hare
pheasant
venison
duck

# Chicken Supreme with Watercress Sauce

**Ingredients**
4 chicken breasts fillets
125 g / 5 oz carrots, cut into fine julienne strips
125 g / 5 oz celery, cut into fine julienne strips
125 g / 5 oz green beans, cut in half, lengthways
4 stalks of tarragon
4 sprigs of fresh tarragon for garnish
salt and freshly ground pepper
Watercress Sauce:
   400 ml / 14 fl oz pt white chicken stock
   100 g / 4 oz watercress leaves
   50 g / 2 oz fromage blanc
   5 tblsp chicken or meat glaze
   salt and freshly ground pepper

**Method**
   Season the chicken breasts with salt and pepper and place in a steamer. Cover with the vegetable strips and tarragon stalks and steam for 4 - 5 minutes. Remove the tarragon stalks and keep the chicken warm.
   Make the sauce by placing 125 ml / 4 fl oz of the chicken stock into a pan with the watercress leaves. Bring to the boil. Allow to cool, then purée in a liquidiser and pass through a nylon sieve. Boil the remaining stock to reduce by half. Whisk the fromage blanc and watercress purée in to the reduced stock. Season to taste.
   Pour the sauce on to four individual plates. Place a chicken breast and vegetable strips carefully into the centre of each plate. Decorate with fresh tarragon.

*Recipe courtesy of The Chiltern Society*


# Anila's Chicken Tikka

**Ingredients**
4 chicken breast fillets
Marinade:
   2 - 3 tblsp natural yoghurt or double cream
   1 tsp lemon juice
   4 tblsp of Anila's Chicken Tikka sauce

**Method**
   Mix well together the ingredients for the marinade and then coat the chicken pieces. Leave for 2 hours, or overnight in a refrigerator.
   Grill the chicken until it is cooked. Serve with naan bread and a tomato and basil salad (p39).

# Chicken and Mushroom Casserole

## Ingredients
1 free-range chicken, approx 1½ kg / 3¼ lb
2 tblsp olive oil
2 medium onions, chopped
4 rashers streaky bacon, diced
400 g / 1lb chestnut mushrooms, chopped
4 carrots, peeled and chopped
4 potatoes, peeled and chopped
2 leeks, chopped
425 ml / ¾ pt chicken stock
fresh herbs - parsley, thyme, fennel, chopped
salt and freshly ground pepper

## Method
Sauté the onion and bacon in half the oil until golden. Add the mushrooms and sauté for a further 5 minutes. Transfer to a casserole dish. Seal the chicken in the remaining oil. Place in the casserole dish. Scatter the chopped vegetables around the meat. Add the herbs, chicken stock and seasoning. Cover and bake at 180°C or gas mark 4 for 1½ - 2 hrs. Remove the poultry from the dish and stand for a few minutes before carving. Serve with the cooked vegetables and gravy.

# Cross Lanes Chicken

## Ingredients
4 chicken quarters
600 g / 1½ lb apples *(Cox's Orange Pippin or similar)*
50 g / 2 oz butter
salt and freshly ground pepper
50 g / 2 oz raisins, soaked in warm water
4 tblsp freshly pressed apple juice *(Cox's Orange Pippin or same as apples)*
1 tblsp lemon juice
150 ml / ¼ pt cream

## Method
Peel and core the apples and slice neatly. Melt half the butter in a frying pan and cook the apple slices on both sides until golden. Put half in the bottom of a casserole dish and reserve the other half. Melt the rest of the butter and brown the chicken quarters, season with salt and pepper and place on top of the apples in the dish. Cover with rest of the apple slices. Pour the apple and lemon juice over, add the raisins and season with salt and pepper.

Cover with greaseproof paper and lid. Cook in oven at 160°C or gas mark 2½ for 1¼ hours. Then stir in the cream and cook for a few minutes until hot.

Serve with new potatoes and green vegetables.

# Poacher's Pot

**Ingredients**
1 rabbit or chicken, 1.5 kg / 2¼ lbs, jointed
2 pigeons, halved
2 grouse or pheasants *(or one of each)*, jointed
1 kg / 2 lbs *(approx)* venison or gammon joint
50 g / 2 oz flour
2 medium sized turnips, peeled and cut into cubes
2 large onions, peeled and sliced
3 large carrots, scraped and cut into rings
4 sprigs fresh thyme
4 sprigs fresh sage
4 sprigs fresh parsley
10 g / ½ oz salt
1 tsp freshly ground black pepper
water for cooking
1 large Savoy cabbage, outer leaves and hard stalk removed, quartered
275 ml / ½ pt red wine

**Method**
Place the meat in a bowl and rub with flour. Put all the vegetables, except the cabbage, in a large saucepan or preserving pan. Place the meat on the top of them. Sprinkle herbs, salt *(if using gammon, only use half the salt)* and pepper over, then, add enough water to cover the meat. Cover pan, bring to the boil, then simmer for 2½ hours. Stir from time to time. After 2 hours add the cabbage and red wine. Make sure that the stock is gently boiling and taste for seasoning. After another ½ hour, take out the venison or gammon, slice, then return to stew to warm through. Serve with mashed potatoes.

# Rabbit Casserole

**Ingredients**
1 rabbit, jointed
salt and freshly ground pepper
plain flour for dusting
30 g / 1¼ oz butter
2 onions, chopped
2 rashers streaky bacon, chopped
30 ml / 2 tblsp brandy
100 ml / 3½ fl oz dry white wine
225 ml / 8 fl oz chicken stock
5 ml / 1 tsp mixed dried herbs
cornflour and water to thicken, if needed

**Method**
Rinse the rabbit in cold water and pat dry with kitchen paper. Sprinkle over some salt and pepper and dust the pieces with flour; shake off the surplus. In a heavy based, flameproof casserole dish melt the butter and add the

chopped onions. Cook over a moderate heat until softened and starting to turn golden. Add the chopped bacon, cook for 5 minutes more, then remove from pan with a slotted spoon. Sauté the rabbit pieces a few at a time over a fairly high heat in the casserole dish, until all sides are slightly coloured. Transfer to a plate with the onions and bacon. Now, keeping the heat fairly high, add the brandy to the casserole dish. Wait 30 seconds, then add the wine and chicken stock. Put the rabbit, bacon and onions back in the dish and sprinkle the mixed herbs over them. Cover and simmer gently over a low heat for 1 - 1½ hrs until tender. Thicken the sauce with the cornflour if needed.

Serve with a selection of fresh vegetables.

# Jugged Hare

**Ingredients**
100 g / 4 oz fine oatmeal
½ tsp each, salt and pepper
1 hare, cleaned, skinned and jointed
75 g / 3 oz butter
1 medium onion, peeled and stuck with cloves
1 large cooking apple, peeled, cored and sliced
225 g / 9 oz mushrooms, cleaned and sliced
1 sprig each, fresh thyme, parsley, marjoram, tied in a bunch
3 bay leaves
1 lemon, sliced
120 ml / 4 fl oz red wine
570 ml / 1 pt beef stock
Forcemeat balls:
   175 g / 7oz breadcrumbs
   50 g / 2 oz shredded suet
   50 g / 2 oz bacon finely chopped and fried until crisp
   2 tsp finely chopped parsley
   3 tsp chopped fresh herbs
   salt and freshly ground black pepper
   1 free-range egg, beaten well
40 g / 1¾ oz butter

**Method**
Season half the oatmeal with the salt and pepper and rub over the hare joints. Heat 50 g / 2 oz of butter in a large frying pan. Add the hare and fry quickly, turning to seal and brown on all sides. Remove from the heat.

Place the hare in large casserole dish, sprinkle with rest of the oatmeal add onions, apple, lemon, mushrooms and herbs. Pour the wine into the stock then into the casserole dish. Cover tightly and stand in a roasting tin. Pour in boiling water to come halfway up the sides of the casserole and cook in the oven at 180°C or gas mark 4 for 3 hours.

Mix all the dry ingredients for the forcemeat balls together, stir in the beaten egg and form into little balls. When the hare is nearly cooked fry the balls in the butter and serve together with the casserole.

# Bodger's Game Pie
*Serves 6*

## Ingredients
Pastry:
   200 g / 8 oz self raising flour
   pinch of salt
   75 g / 3 oz good-quality cooking fat
   25 g / 1oz unsalted butter
   1 free-range egg
   a little chilled milk
Filling:
   550 g / 1¼ lb mixed game - venison, rabbit, hare, pheasant - cubed
   1 bottle / ½ pint *'Bodgers'* or a strong barley wine *(Chiltern Brewery)*
   25 g / 1 oz seasoned flour
   2 fine-quality British pork sausages
   50 g / 2 oz dry cured smoked streaky bacon, diced
   25 g / 1 oz dripping for cooking
   100 g / 4 oz chicken thighs, boned and cubed
   1 large onion, chopped, 1 large carrot, diced, 1 stick celery, sliced
   6 juniper berries
   good meat or game stock

## Method
    Place the cubed game in a glass dish, pour over the barley wine, and marinate in the fridge overnight. The next day, place a sieve over a bowl and drain the game through it, saving the liquid. Blot the game dry and toss lightly in seasoned flour.
    Heat the dripping in a frying pan and add diced bacon and sausages, frying briefly to brown on all sides and release fat. Remove to a heavy pan or casserole with a slotted spoon, cutting the sausages into chunks. Fry the game a little at a time to seal quickly on all sides, then add it to the pan or casserole. Add the chicken, onion, carrot, celery and juniper berries to the pan, then pour over the barley wine marinade, adding around ¼ litre / ½ pt stock, to cover all the ingredients. Cook very slowly in the oven at 150°C or gas mark 2 for 2 hours until the meat is tender but still has a little bite.
    As soon as the filling starts cooking, make the pastry. Lightly rub the fat into the sifted flour and salt until it resembles fine breadcrumbs. Whisk the egg and stir in a very little milk, then make a well in the centre of the flour mixture and pour in the egg and milk, reserving around 1 tblsp to glaze the pie. Mix together, adding enough cold milk to make a soft, but not sloppy pastry. Wrap in cling film and chill for 2 hours.
    Remove from the fridge and bring back to room temperature. Pour the game mixture into a pie bowl and allow to cool slightly while the oven heats to 220°C, gas mark 7. Roll out the pastry on a floured board and cover the pie, crimping the edges and brushing with retained egg /milk. Bake towards the top of the oven for 30 minutes until the filling is bubbling and the pastry crisp and golden brown.
    Serve with mashed potato and swede or braised red cabbage.

*Reproduced by permission of Mrs S Nowak, The Beer Cook Book 1999, ISBN 0-571-19219-X*

# Roast Venison

Conventional roasting of a joint of venison *(haunch or saddle)* is better suited to a fast roast method, which leaves the meat a little rare and still moist. First brown the joint all over in hot oil, then roast in a pre-heated oven at 230°C or gas mark 8 for 26 minutes per kg or 12 minutes per lb. Rest the meat in a warm oven for about 15 minutes. Carve thinly.

# Pot-roast Venison

### Ingredients
1.5 kg / 3 lb *(approx)* venison joint - haunch, saddle or shoulder
1 onion, skinned and chopped
3 carrots, chopped
2 leeks, thoroughly washed and chopped
2 parsnips, chopped
1.2 litres / 2 pints stock
fresh herbs, chopped
salt and freshly ground pepper
2 tblsp redcurrant jelly

### Method
Put half of the chopped vegetables into a casserole, or pot-roast dish. Place the meat on the top, put the rest of the vegetables around it. Add the stock, herbs and seasoning.

Cook in a medium oven at 160°C or gas mark 2½ for about 2 hours until the meat is tender. Remove the meat and carve in thick slices. Cover with the drained vegetables. Thicken the remaining juices, add the redcurrant jelly and serve as gravy.

# Blackcurrant Venison Steaks

### Ingredients
4 venison steaks
salt and freshly ground black pepper
1 large onion, skinned and finely chopped
1 tblsp cooking oil
150 g / 6 oz blackcurrants
2 tblsp water
a little sugar

### Method
Heat the oil in a frying pan and quickly brown the seasoned steaks on both sides. Reduce the heat and add the onion. Continue frying for a further 10 minutes, turning the steaks once.

Cook the blackcurrants with a little water, sweeten to taste. Transfer the steaks from the pan to a dish. Add the cooked blackcurrants and their liquid to the fried onions. Heat the mixture through and pour over the steaks.

Serve with new potatoes and a fresh green salad.

## Venison Casserole

**Ingredients**
900 g / 2 lb diced shoulder of venison
150 ml / ¼ pt port, or red wine
2 tblsp cooking oil
1 tblsp flour
salt and freshly ground pepper
2 onions
6 sticks of celery
3 carrots
mixed fresh herbs, chopped
570 ml / 1 pt stock

**Method**
    Marinate the meat in the port or wine for 24 hours. Drain and dry the meat. Coat in the flour and seasoning and brown in 1 tblsp of oil over a high heat. Remove from the pan and place in a casserole dish.
    Finely slice all the vegetables, turn down the heat and fry gently in the remaining oil for 3 minutes. Add these to the casserole dish together with the rest of the ingredients, including the marinade liquid. Cook at 160°C or gas mark 2½ for two and a half hours, until tender.
    Serve with mashed potatoes and green vegetables.

## Chinese Crispy Duck with Plum Sauce

**Ingredients**
2.2 kg / 5 lb duck
Sauce:
    400 g / 1 lb plums
    2 tblsp water
    2 tblsp tomato paste
    2 tblsp demerara sugar
    2 tblsp clear English honey
    1 tblsp red wine vinegar
    1½ tsp Chinese 5 spice seasoning
    1 clove garlic, skinned and crushed
    salt and freshly ground black pepper

**Method**
    Halve and stone the plums. Cook gently in a little water until soft. Reserve the cooking liquid and place the plums in a blender with the other sauce ingredients. Purée until smooth. Mix the purée with about three tblsp of the reserved plum juice.
    Prick the duck all over to let the fat run out during cooking. Place the duck on a trivet in a roasting tin and brush generously with the plum sauce. Roast in the oven for about 1½ hrs at 190°C or gas mark 5, basting at intervals, until crisp and golden.
    Carve and serve with the remaining sauce, thinned with any remaining juice if necessary. Serve with baked sliced potatoes (p33) and vegetables.

# MEAT

beef
lamb
pork
ostrich

## Traditional Roast Beef

Highland beef is characterised by fat marbled through it; this ensures it stays moist during cooking and gives it a unique flavour. Joints suitable for roasting include sirloin, topside or forerib. Allow about 150 g / 6 oz meat per person. Pre heat the oven to 220°C or gas mark 7 and roast for 45 minutes per kg / 20 minutes per lb plus 20 minutes extra. Serve with thin gravy, horseradish sauce or mustard. Roast potatoes, parsnips and vegetables are the usual accompaniments and don't forget the Yorkshire puddings made with free-range eggs from the Farmers' Market!

*The following Highland Beef recipes are reproduced by kind permission of the Highland Cattle Society and Highland Drovers.*

## Highland Brisket with Creamy Mustard and Caramelised Shallot Sauce

### Ingredients
1 kg / 2 ¼ lb joint Highland Beef brisket
Marinade:
  1 bottle of white wine
  sprig of rosemary
  slice or two of carrot
  slice or two of onion
*Place the brisket in a casserole dish and pour over the marinade and leave in the refrigerator for at least 12 hours, turning occasionally*
1 large onion, chopped
oil for cooking
125 ml / 5 fl of double cream
1 tblsp of cornflour
75 ml / 3 fl oz whole grain mustard
500 g / 1lb 2 oz of shallots, peeled
1 tblsp of golden syrup

### Method
   Heat a little oil in a frying pan and cook the onions until soft. Remove from the pan and reserve. Lift the brisket from the marinade, pat dry with a paper towel. Brown the joint on all sides in the pan where the onions were cooked. Put the brisket, the onions and the marinade in a casserole dish. Cover and cook in a pre-heated oven for 2 hours at 180°C or gas mark 4.
   Meanwhile, cook the shallots in a little oil until soft and brown. Finally stir in the golden syrup and put to one side. When the brisket is cooked, remove from its dish and keep warm on a serving plate. Strain the cooking liquid through a sieve. A generous pint is needed for the sauce, so if there is extra, return to a pan and reduce by boiling. Add the cream and stir, returning to the heat, but do not boil.
   Mix the cornflour with two tablespoons of cold water and add to the sauce to thicken. Finally stir in the mustard. Add the caramelised shallots and simmer gently for a few minutes until the sauce darkens slightly. Cut the brisket into thick slices and pour over the sauce. Serve with vegetables in season.

# Pot-roast Topside Highland Beef with Root Vegetables

## Ingredients
900 g / 2 lb piece of rolled topside Highland beef
150 g / 6 oz smoked streaky bacon, chopped
1 carrot, peeled and chopped
75 g / 3 oz celeriac, peeled and diced
2 cloves of garlic, skinned and crushed
1 tblsp plain flour
125 ml / 4 fl oz red wine
225 ml / 8 fl oz beef stock
1 bouquet garni, or fresh herbs - parsley, bay, marjoram, thyme and rosemary
½ tsp tomato purée
salt and freshly ground black pepper
Garnish:
  1 carrot
  75 g / 3 oz celeriac
  75 g / 3 oz turnip
  75 g / 3 oz baby onions
  chopped fresh parsley

## Method
Put the beef in a heavy based flameproof casserole dish and fry over a medium heat until browned on all sides. The fat around the joint should be sufficient for frying.

Remove the meat from the pot and set aside. Put the bacon in the casserole and gently heat until the fat runs. Increase the heat and cook until the bacon is crisp. Lift out with a slotted spoon and set aside with the beef. Lower the heat and add the prepared vegetables to the casserole. Place the lid on and allow them to soften. Continue to cook until they are lightly coloured, then add the flour and *stir*. Gradually add the wine, tomato purée and stock. Bring the sauce slowly to the boil, stirring occasionally, to achieve a smooth sauce.

Return the bacon and topside to the pan, add the bouquet garni and some salt and pepper. Cover and cook in a pre-heated oven at 180°C or gas mark 4, for 1- 2 hours, or until the beef is tender when pierced with a knife.

Meanwhile prepare the garnish. Cut the carrot, celeriac and turnip into neat baton shapes. Peel the baby onions. Cook all these vegetables together in a frying pan with a little water, butter and sugar. *(The idea is that when the vegetables are cooked, all the water is absorbed and the butter and sugar form a glaze around the vegetables.)* When the meat is cooked transfer to a carving dish and rest for 15 minutes at room temperature before carving.

While the meat is resting, strain the cooking liquid, removing any surface fat, and pour into a wide saucepan. Bring to the boil and reduce until the desired consistency and intensity of flavour is reached.

To serve, reheat the vegetable garnish and divide between warmed serving plates. Carve the topside and place slices on top of the glazed root vegetables. Coat with the sauce and sprinkle with parsley.

## Highland Escalopes with Fresh Tomatoes, Black Olives and Basil

### Ingredients
4 medium escalopes of beef
2 tblsp olive oil
1 clove of garlic, skinned and finely chopped
4 tomatoes, skinned, deseeded and cut in wedges
4 - 6 black olives, stoned and cut into chunks
fresh basil leaves, roughly chopped
425 ml / ¾ pt beef stock
salt and freshly ground black pepper

### Method
    In a large frying pan heat the olive oil and brown the escalopes well on each side. Transfer them to a warm dish, and keep then warm. Add the garlic to the frying pan, and cook for a minute or two, then add the tomatoes, olives and beef stock. Season with salt and pepper and let the liquid bubble away until it has reduced by about half. Stir in the basil, and pour over the escalopes in the warm dish. Serve with new potatoes and green vegetables.

## Casserole of Highland Beef with Prunes and Pickled Walnuts

### Ingredients
525 g /1lb 5 oz lean stewing steak cut into chunks
2 tblsp plain flour
salt and freshly ground black pepper
4 tblsps sunflower oil
2 medium onions, skinned and sliced thinly
1 clove of garlic, skinned and finely chopped
1 jar pickled walnuts, drained of their liquid and the walnuts chopped
125 g / 6 oz cooked and stoned prunes *(retain the liquid)*
570 ml / 1 pint water or 275 ml / ½ pt water and 275 ml / ½ pt red wine

### Method
    Heat the oil in a heavy-based, flameproof casserole dish. Toss the pieces of meat in the seasoned flour, and brown them, a small amount at a time, in the hot oil. When they are brown, remove them from the casserole and keep them warm. When all the meat is browned, lower the heat and add the sliced onions to the casserole dish. Cook for about 5 minutes, stirring occasionally so that they cook evenly. Add the chopped garlic, and any remaining seasoned flour. Stir and cook for a minute or two, then stir in the water, or water and wine, the prunes and their cooking liquid and the pickled walnuts. Stir until the sauce boils, replace the browned meat in the casserole, bring to simmering point again, cover with a lid, and cook in a moderate oven, 180° C or gas mark 4, for 1½ hours.

# Highland Beef Pilaff

**Ingredients**
600 g / 1½ lb minced Highland beef
25 g / 1 oz butter
1 large onion, peeled and chopped
3 cloves of garlic, crushed
2 tsp ground coriander
1 tsp cumin
½ tsp turmeric
2.5 cm / 1in piece of ginger root, peeled and grated
1 cinnamon stick, broken into chunks
1 tsp tomato purée
570 ml / 1 pt chicken stock
salt and freshly ground black pepper
200 g / 8 oz frozen peas *(defrosted)*
300 g / 12 oz long grain rice
50 g / 2 oz seedless raisins
50 g / 2 oz pine kernels
1 bunch of coriander leaves, chopped

**Method**
   Melt the butter in a large flame-proof casserole. Add the onion and fry gently until soft. Add the garlic and the minced beef, turn up the heat and brown, stirring well. Add the spices and the ginger root and continue cooking for a few minutes. Then stir in the tomato purée and 150 ml / ¼ pt of the chicken stock. Season and bring to the boil, stirring. Lower the heat, cover and simmer for 1 hour until the meat is tender.
   Add the remaining stock to the casserole, bring to the boil, then add the rice. Stir well, cover and simmer gently for about 15 minutes until the rice is cooked and all the stock absorbed. Fold in the peas, raisins and pine kernels and heat through for a few minutes. Adjust the seasoning and sprinkle with chopped coriander leaves.
   Serve with garlic bread and a side salad.

# Adrienne's Beef and Mushroom Casserole

**Ingredients**
900 g / 2 lb topside of beef, cut into thin strips
1 tblsp oil
2 medium onions, chopped
4 rashers of streaky bacon, chopped
400 g / 1 lb mushrooms, chopped
4 large carrots, chopped
275 ml / ½ pt strong ale *(Chiltern Brewery)*
275 ml / ½ pt beef stock
fresh herbs - parsley, thyme, bay, chopped
salt and freshly ground pepper

**Method**
    Sauté the onion and bacon in the oil until golden. Transfer to a casserole dish. Seal the beef strips quickly. Add these to the casserole, together with the carrots, herbs, seasoning, ale and stock. Cover and cook for 1½ hrs at 180°C or gas mark 4. Add the mushrooms and cook for further 20 minutes. Serve with boiled potatoes and spring greens.

# Spiced Highland Meatballs
*This makes about 25 - 30 meatballs*

**Ingredients**
400 g / 1 lb lean minced beef
1 medium onion, skinned and finely chopped
1 tblsp chopped parsley
25g / 1 oz fresh white or brown breadcrumbs
pinch of salt and freshly ground black pepper
1 tsp medium curry powder
1 dstsp mango chutney
plain flour in which to roll the meatballs
oil for frying

**Method**
    In a food processor whisk together all the above ingredients. Make the mixture into small balls about the size of a walnut, and roll each in flour. Shallow fry in the oil, turning them over so that they cook and brown evenly. Drain the matballs on some kitchen paper to absorb any excess grease.
*These are delicious hot, or cold with the following recipes for dips:*
**1. Pickle and Whipped Cream**
Fold together 275 ml / ½ pt whipped cream and 1 tblsp pickle.
**2. Tomato and Horseradish Sauce**
Mix 275 ml / ½ pt liquidised homemade tomato sauce, with 2 tsp horseradish sauce stirred through it.

# Beefburger Whopper

**Ingredients**
4 ready prepared beefburgers
4 round burger buns
grated cheese
1 onion, skinned and sliced
4 tblsp tomato relish *(see p 86)*
crisp lettuce, thinly shredded

**Method**
    Grill the burgers until they are cooked through. Fry the onions in a little oil until they are soft and golden. Slit the burger buns in two and lightly toast the outsides. Place the cooked burger in the bun base. Top with the cheese, fried onions, relish and shredded lettuce. Cover with the lid of the bun.

## Traditional Roast Lamb

Lamb joints suitable for roasting include leg or shoulder. For meat on the bone allow 300 g / ¾ lb of meat per person. For cuts off the bone about 150 g / 6 oz meat per person. Pre-heat the oven to 190°C or gas mark 5 and roast for 55 minutes per kg / 25 minutes per lb, plus 25 minutes extra. Serve with thin gravy, apple and mint jelly, or redcurrant jelly, onion sauce and a selection of roasted and boiled vegetables.

## Colin's Lamb Casserole

**Ingredients**
900 g / 2 lb lean diced lamb *(taken from the leg)*
175 g / 7 oz carrots, peeled and chopped
175 g / 7 oz turnips, peeled and chopped
175 g / 7 oz onions, skinned and chopped
1½ tblsp oil
1½ tblsp flour
1½ tblsp tomato purée
150 ml / ¼ pt unsweetened orange juice
150 ml / ¼ pt stock
125 g / 5 oz button mushrooms
1 bay leaf
salt and freshly ground pepper
Choux pastry:
    50 g / 2 oz butter
    150 ml / ¼ pt water
    65 g / 2½ oz plain flour
    pinch of salt
    2 free-range eggs, lightly beaten
    2 tblsp fresh parsley, chopped

**Method**
Heat the oil in a large pan. Add the diced lamb together with the chopped vegetables and stir over a high heat for 2 - 3 minutes. Add the flour and the tomato purée. Cook, stirring, for a further 2 minutes. Add the orange juice, stock and bay leaf. Bring to the boil. Season to taste.

Transfer to a casserole dish, cover and bake at 180°C or gas mark 4 for 1½ hours until the meat is tender. Stir in the mushrooms and transfer everything into a 1.8 litre / 3 pt ovenproof dish. Allow to get cold.

Make the choux pastry by first sifting the flour and the salt. Melt the butter slowly in the water, bring to the boil, then add the flour and salt. Immediately take off the heat, beat well until the paste forms a ball and leaves the sides of the pan. Turn into a bowl and cool slightly. Beat in the eggs one at a time, keeping the mixture stiff.

Beat the chopped parsley into the choux pastry mixture. Spoon over the lamb and bake at 200°C or gas mark 6 for 1 hour, until the choux is risen and golden.

# Country Lamb Stew

### Ingredients
4 lamb chops
15 g / ¾ oz butter or oil
300 g / 12 oz new potatoes, cut in half
200 g / 8 oz small onions, skinned and chopped
400 g / 1 lb chopped chestnut mushrooms
150 ml / ¼ pt white wine
250 ml / 9 fl oz stock
salt and freshly ground pepper
a bay leaf & sprig each of thyme, parsley and marjoram, tied in a bunch
parsley for garnish

### Method
   Sauté the lamb chops in the hot butter or oil to seal them on both sides. Add the potatoes, onions and mushrooms to the pan and cook for 5 minutes. Add the wine and the stock, herbs and seasoning. Cover the pan and simmer for 1 hour. Remove the bunch of herbs. Garnish with parsley. Serve with mashed potatoes and carrots.

# Spring into Summer Stew

### Ingredients
400 g / 1 lb lean lamb, cubed
1 finely shredded, crisp lettuce
150 g / 6 oz shelled green peas
50 g / 2 oz spring onions, chopped
125 ml / 4 fl oz stock
½ tsp sugar
salt and freshly ground pepper
125 g / 5 oz cucumber, peeled and sliced
250 g / 10 oz button mushrooms

### Method
Put the lamb, lettuce, peas, onions, stock, sugar, salt and pepper into a pan. Cover and cook gently for 1½ hours. Add the mushrooms and the cucumber and cook for a further half an hour. Serve on a bed of plain boiled rice.

# Minced Lamb Curry

### Ingredients
1 bottle Anila's Medium or Mild Curry sauce
600 g / 1½ lb lamb, minced
1 onion, chopped
2 medium potatoes, peeled and cut into large cubes
275 ml / ½ pt water
fresh coriander, chopped *(for garnish)*
2 tomatoes

## Method
Pour the sauce into a pan and heat gently. Add the onion and the minced lamb and cook for 5 minutes. Add the cubed potatoes, then add the water and cook for 15 minutes. Sprinkle with chopped coriander and wedges of tomato. Serve on a bed of plain boiled rice.

# Foxbury Noisettes

## Ingredients
2 lamb noisettes per person
butter and oil for frying
Sauce:
   1 carrot and 1 onion, diced
   2 sticks of celery, diced
   25 g / 1 oz bacon, diced
   50 g / 2 oz butter
   1 tblsp tomato purée
   25 g / 1 oz flour
   1 - 2 tblsp of redcurrant jelly
   125 ml / 4 fl oz brown stock
   275 ml / ½ pt red wine
   bouquet garni
   salt and freshly ground pepper

## Method
Fry the diced vegetables and bacon in 50 g / 2 oz of butter until golden. Add the tomato purée and flour to make a roux. Gradually blend in the stock and wine. Season to taste and add the bouquet garni. Simmer in a saucepan with the lid on for 30 minutes. Strain and add the redcurrant jelly to the sauce.
   Fry the lamb noisettes in butter and oil for 4 - 6 minutes on each side until well browned, but still pink inside. Serve the noisettes with the sauce poured over them, with new potatoes, courgettes and beans.

# Berkshire Barbeque Lamb Steaks

## Ingredients
4 large lamb chump chops or steaks
Marinade:
   1 tblsp fresh mint leaves, finely chopped
   1 medium onion, skinned and finely chopped
   60 ml / 2½ fl oz medium sherry
   30 ml / 1¼ fl oz olive oil
   1 clove of garlic, skinned and crushed
   salt and freshly ground pepper

## Method
Using a food processor, blend the mint and onion until smooth. add the remaining marinade ingredients and mix completely until thick. Put the lamb steaks in a dish and cover with the marinade. Cover and leave in a refrigerator overnight.
   Cook the meat on a medium barbeque for 5 - 7 minutes on each side, basting with the marinade. Serve with a fresh green salad and crusty bread.

## Roast Pork

Pork joints suitable for roasting include loin or leg . For meat on the bone allow 300 g / ¾ lb per person. For cuts off the bone about 150 g / 6 oz meat per person. Pre heat the oven to 220°C or gas mark 7 and roast for 55 minutes per kg / 25 minutes per lb, plus 25 minutes extra. To make crackling on roast pork, score the uncooked rind with a sharp knife, brush with oil and sprinkle with salt. Serve with thick gravy, apple or gooseberry sauce and a selection of roasted and boiled vegetables.

## Caribbean Pork Jerk

**Ingredients**
1.2 kg / 3 lb rolled spare rib joint or diced pork
3 pork belly slices, skinned and diced
Marinade:
   3 tblsp lemon juice
   2 tblsp balsamic vinegar
   1 tsp Jamaican Jerk spices
   ½ tsp Jamaican pepper *(ground allspice)*
   1 tsp lemon pepper
   1 fresh garlic clove, crushed
   2 tsp brown sugar
   1 tsp salt
   1 small red chilli
   1 small green chilli
1 courgette, chopped
1 red pepper, deseeded and chopped
1 green pepper, deseeded and chopped
1 tin chickpeas, strained
1 lb skinned fresh tomatoes, chopped or 1 tin of chopped tomatoes
275 ml / ½ pint of pork or chicken stock

**Method**
Blend together the ingredients for the marinade. Place the meat in a large container and cover with the marinade. Marinate for at least 2 hours.
Heat a little oil in a large saucepan. Add the meat, stirring all the time to seal, then add the tomatoes and half of the stock. Cover the pan, bring to the boil and then simmer over a low heat for 1 – 1½ hours until the meat is tender. *(Alternatively, if using an ovenproof dish, transfer to an oven and cook for the same time at 170°C or gas mark 3.)* Check the pan during this time to ensure that there is enough moisture, and, if necessary add more of the stock.
For the last half-hour of cooking add the peppers, courgette and chickpeas. Adjust the seasoning and serve with rice or crusty bread.

# Pork Wellington

**Ingredients**
1 pork tenderloin
1 packet of ready-made puff pastry
1 free-range egg, beaten
75 g / 3 oz of sage and onion stuffing mix
250 ml / 9 fl oz of boiling water
75 g / 3 oz moist marinated sun-dried tomatoes
75g / 3 oz mushrooms, chopped
oil or butter for greasing

**Method**
　　Place the tenderloin on a baking tray, brush with a little oil or butter and bake at 190° C or gas mark 5 for 20 - 30 minutes. Remove from the oven. In the meantime, soak the sage and onion stuffing with the boiling water and allow to cool.
　　Roll out pastry twice the length and just over the width of the tenderloin. Grease another baking tray and lightly dust with flour. Place the pastry on the tray. Place the cooled sage and onion stuffing on half the length of pastry, spreading as evenly as possible to match the size of the tenderloin. Place the tenderloin on top of the stuffing and then cover the top and sides with the sun-dried tomatoes and mushrooms. Moisten edges of pastry all the way round and fold the pastry over the meat and vegetables. Seal the edges and trim neatly. Brush with the beaten egg and place in the oven to bake for approximately 30 minutes until it is golden brown.

# Fruity Pork Curry

**Ingredients**
900 g / 2 lb cubed lean pork
2 medium onions, finely chopped
1 tblsp oil
2 - 3 tsp mild curry paste
2 dessert apples *(Cox's Orange Pippin, or similar)*, peeled and diced
2 tblsp sultanas
1 tblsp plain flour
4 tblsp mango chutney
1 pint chicken stock
2 tblsp sour cream or coconut milk
a handful of washed green seedless grapes

**Method**
　　Fry the onions in the oil until softened. Add the pork and seal it. Add the curry paste and continue frying until the meat is coated. Stir in the apples, mango chutney and sultanas. Sprinkle the flour over the mixture and continue cooking for 1 - 2 minutes. Cover with the chicken stock and stir the ingredients until they are well amalgamated. Bring to the boil, then simmer over a gentle heat until for 45 minutes - 1 hour until tender. Add the grapes and the cream or coconut milk. Re-heat before serving, but do not boil. Serve on a bed of plain boiled rice.

## Pork and Mushrooms

**Ingredients**
4 lean pork chops
15 g / ¾ oz butter
150 g / 6 oz leeks, washed and chopped
250 g / 10 oz button mushrooms
1 tblsp flour
425 ml / ¾ pt strong ale (*Chiltern Brewery*)
salt and freshly ground pepper
1 bay leaf
pared rind of ½ lemon

**Method**
Brown the chops in the butter. Transfer to an ovenproof casserole dish together with the leeks and the mushrooms. Stir the flour into the remaining melted butter, cook and gradually add the ale. Bring to the boil, stirring until thickened. Season with the salt and pepper. Pour the liquid over the chops and vegetables. Add the bay leaf and lemon rind and cover and cook for 40 minutes at 160°C or gas mark 2½. Serve with mashed potatoes and vegetables in season.

## Pork Escalopes with Stir-fry Red Cabbage and Prunes

**Ingredients**
8 lean pork escalopes
2 onions, skinned and chopped
4 rashers of streaky bacon, chopped
3 apples (*Bramley or similar*), peeled, cored and chopped
400 g / 1 lb red cabbage, shredded
16 prunes, stoned and chopped
8 dstsp white wine vinegar
salt and freshly ground pepper

**Method**
Heat the oil in a wok, or large frying pan and fry the bacon until it is crisp. Add the onion and sauté lightly for a few minutes. Add the cabbage and stir-fry for three minutes. Stir in the apples and the prunes, vinegar and seasonings. Stir fry for a further ten minutes. Season the pork and fry gently in another pan until golden brown on both sides. Serve with the fruit and vegetable stir-fry and hot crusty bread.

## Cheesy Pork Steaks

**Ingredients**
4 pork steaks
1 tblsp of olive oil
salt and freshly ground pepper
450 g / 1 lb 2oz fresh tomatoes, skinned or 1 tin of tomatoes
2 tsp fresh herbs, finely chopped
150 g / 6 oz Cheddar cheese, grated
150 g / 6 oz fresh white breadcrumbs

## Method

Season the pork steaks and fry in the olive oil for 3 minutes each side. Remove and place in an ovenproof dish.

Mix the tomatoes with the herbs and place over and around the pork steaks. Mix three-quarters of the cheese with the breadcrumbs and spread evenly over the top of the steaks. Sprinkle the top with the remaining cheese and bake in the centre of the oven at 180°C or gas mark 4 for 15 minutes until the cheese has melted to a golden colour.

Serve with new potatoes and fresh green vegetables.

# Pork Mince Stir-fry

## Ingredients

400 g / 1 lb pork mince
1 onion or 1 bunch of spring onions
1 medium courgette
2 medium carrots
1 red pepper, deseeded
1 green pepper, deseeded
1 garlic clove, crushed
2 tblsp tomato sauce
2 tblsp soy sauce

## Method

Prepare vegetables by cutting them into long thin strips. In a wok or large frying pan, fry the mince for 2 - 3 minutes. Add the crushed garlic and fry on a high heat for 1 minute. Add the prepared vegetables and stir-fry until they have just softened. Remove from the heat and stir in the tomato and soy sauces. Return to the heat and stir well to coat evenly. Serve with boiled rice.

# Pork and Macaroni Casserole

## Ingredients

100 g / 4 oz macaroni
300 g / 12 oz minced lean pork
1 small onion, skinned and chopped
1 small green pepper, deseeded and chopped
125 g / 5 oz celery, chopped
½ clove garlic, crushed
1 small can of tomatoes
75 g / 3 oz tomato purée
1 bay leaf
1 dstsp fresh chopped parsley
pinch of paprika
salt and freshly ground pepper
oil for frying
Sauce:
   10 g / ½ oz butter
   1 tblsp plain flour
   425 ml / ¾ pt milk
   3 spring onions, chopped
   1 free-range egg yolk, beaten

50 g / 2 oz Cheddar Cheese, grated
  1 tblsp 'English style' Parmesan cheese, grated
  125 g / 5 oz shelled peas
Garnish:
  cherry tomatoes
  parsley

### Method

Heat some oil in a pan and brown the minced pork for 5 - 10 minutes. Add the onions, green pepper, celery and garlic and cook for a further 10 - 15 minutes, stirring frequently. Drain and return to the pan with the undrained tomatoes, tomato purée, bay leaf, parsley, salt, pepper and paprika. Stir and bring to the boil. Reduce the heat and simmer for 40 minutes, stirring occasionally.

Cook the macaroni in boiling salted water, according to the instructions on the packet, and drain.

Melt the butter in a heavy saucepan, add the flour and stir until smooth. Cook for 1 minute, stirring throughout. Gradually add the milk, stirring continuously over a medium heat, until slightly thickened and bubbling. Add the spring onions and cook for a further minute. Add a quarter of the sauce to the beaten egg yolks and stir well. Add the remainder and stir in. Add both cheeses, the macaroni and peas and mix well. Spoon the macaroni mixture around the sides of a 1.2 litre / 2 pt casserole dish and spoon the pork mixture into the centre of the dish. Bake at 180°C or gas mark 4 for approximately 20 minutes. Garnish with cherry tomatoes and parsley.

## Sausages in Cider

### Ingredients
400 g / 1 lb British pork sausages
100 g / 4 oz streaky bacon
1 tblsp cooking oil
1 large onion, skinned and chopped
1 English cooking apple *(Bramley, or similar)*
200 g / ½ lb mushrooms, peeled and chopped
25 g / 1 oz flour
sprig of fresh sage
salt and freshly ground pepper
275 ml / ½ pt dry cider or apple juice

### Method

Heat the oil in a large frying pan and brown the sausages on all sides. Remove and keep warm. Chop the bacon, onions and mushrooms and fry over a high heat for 5 minutes. Sprinkle on the flour, salt and pepper, then add the cider, or apple juice, stirring all the time *(it may foam and sizzle, so make sure the pan is large enough)*.

Peel, core and chop the apple and add that, together with the sage and browned sausages, to the fried vegetables. Cover and simmer over a gentle heat for 30 minutes, taking care that it does not dry out. Add more cider if necessary.

Serve with mashed potatoes and fresh green vegetables.

# Barbeque Sausages with Apple and Orange Sauce

### Ingredients
6 British pork sausages
Marinade:
   2 tblsp of clear English honey
   2 tblsp olive oil
   4 tblsp white wine
   2 cloves of garlic, crushed
   1½ tsp cumin
Sauce:
   400 g / 1lb English cooking apples *(Bramleys or Russets)*
   25 g / 1 oz butter
   4 tblsp orange juice
   2 - 3 tblsp marmalade

### Method
   Combine the honey, oil, wine, garlic and cumin and stir well. Put the sausages in a shallow dish and cover in the marinade. Leave for several hours, or overnight, turning occasionally.
   To make the sauce, peel, core and slice the apples and cook in the butter and orange juice until soft and fluffy. Mash, then stir in the marmalade. Re-heat, but do not boil.
   Barbeque, grill or fry the meat and serve with the hot sauce.

# Special Toad-in-the-Hole

### Ingredients
400 g / 1 lb pork, apple and leek sausages
4 rashers of streaky dry cure bacon, cut into bits
Batter:
   150 g / 6 oz plain flour
   pinch of salt
   2 large free-range eggs
   570 ml / 1 pint - milk and water mixed
2 tblsp oil

### Method
   Prepare the batter an hour early. Put the flour and salt into a bowl. Make a well in the centre, break the eggs into it and beat them into the flour, slowly adding the milk and water mix until a smooth batter consistency is reached. Beat well, cover and leave to stand.
   Pre-heat the oven to 220°C or gas mark 7. Prick the sausages. Put the oil in a frying pan and sear the sausages in the hot oil until they are evenly brown. Remove the sausages and put to one side. Pour the oil from the frying pan into an ovenproof dish and place in the oven to heat through. Pour the batter onto the hot oil. Place the browned sausages in the batter and scatter the bacon on the top. Return to the oven. When the batter is puffed and golden, turn the oven temperature down to 190°C or gas mark 5. Total cooking time should be between 35 - 40 minutes.
   Served with mashed potatoes, boiled carrots and onion gravy (see *p66*).

## Gammon Cooked in Ale and Caramelised in Mash Tun Marmalade
*Serves around 20 as a buffet centrepiece*

### Ingredients
2¼ - 4½ kg / 5 -10 lb gammon joint, green or smoked *(Gammon on the bone looks impressive, but boneless is easier to carve in round slices)*
1 medium onion, peeled and left whole
1 large carrot, peeled and left whole
1.2 litres / 2 pints full-bodied bitter beer
water
Mash Tun Marmalade *(containing Chiltern Brewery dark roasted malt)*

### Method
    Place gammon in large pan or casserole. Pour over between 600 ml and 1.2 litres / 1-2 pints beer, depending on the size, and top up with water to three-quarters cover. Add the onion and carrot, then bring very slowly to simmering point; skim off any scum. Cover and simmer very gently for 45 minutes to 1 hour for smaller joints, up to 2 hours for larger, then remove from heat and leave to cool in the liquor. Remove the joint, discarding onion and carrot, but not the stock *(it makes the best pea soup in the world!)*. Leave to dry naturally; remove rind and score the fat. Heat oven to 230°C or gas mark 8, place the gammon in roasting tray and spread sparingly with the marmalade, including the bits of peel. Place in oven for up to 30 minutes, depending on size, until the marmalade caramelises to a dark, glossy veneer.
    Leave overnight to go cold and ready to carve into slices with a bitter / sweet edge.
*Recipe reproduced by permission of Mrs S Nowak, The Beer Cook Book 1999,.ISBN 0-571-19219-X*

## Redman's Bacon and Pineapple Stir-fry

### Ingredients
300 g / 12 oz unsmoked back bacon, cut into 2½ cm / 1 in pieces
1 carrot, cut into julienne strips
100 g / 4 oz beansprouts
1 small can of pineapple pieces in natural juice *(reserve juice)*
1 tsp oil
Sauce:
    1 tblsp tomato ketchup
    1 tsp clear English honey
    1 tsp soy sauce
    1 tsp malt vinegar
    2 tsp cornflour

### Method
    Heat the oil in a wok or large frying pan. Add the bacon and cook for 3-4 minutes until browned. Drain off any excess liquid. Add the carrot strips and cook for 2 minutes. Add the beansprouts and the pineapple pieces.
    Mix together the ingredients for the sauce and and add the reserved pineapple juice. Stir thoroughly and pour into the wok. Stir-fry for a further 3 minutes until the ingredients are coated in the sauce. Serve with rice noodles.

# Ostrich Fillet Steaks with Mushroom Sauce

## Ingredients
4 ostrich fillet steaks
4 tblsp Worcestershire sauce
½ tsp garlic purée or fresh garlic, crushed
salt and freshly ground pepper to taste
4 large mushrooms,
8 shallots or 1 medium red onion
275 ml / ½ pt red wine
pinch of salt, freshly ground pepper
ground nutmeg
olive oil

## Method
    Preheat the grill. Mix the Worcestershire sauce and the seasonings together and dip the steaks in until well coated. Grill the steaks under a medium heat, until cooked to your liking.
    Meanwhile, finely chop the mushrooms and the shallots or onions and sauté in the olive oil. Add the red wine, salt, pepper and nutmeg. Simmer for 2 minutes. Pour the sauce immediately over the cooked ostrich steaks.
    Serve with new potatoes, or mashed potatoes according to season, and a selection of fresh vegetables.

# Ostrich Hotpot

## Ingredients
400 g / 1 lb diced ostrich steak
1 large red onion
2 large carrots
1 medium parsnip or turnip
2 medium potatoes
50 g / 2 oz pearl barley
2 bay leaves
1 tblsp flour
1 tblsp cornflour
570 ml / 1 pt chicken stock
2 tblsp Worcestershire sauce
salt and freshly ground pepper to taste
oil for cooking

## Method
    Pre-heat the oven to 150°C or gas mark 2. Mix together the flour, cornflour and seasonings and coat the steak. Heat the oil in a frying pan and lightly fry the steak until sealed, then place in a large casserole dish. Chop and dice the vegetables and place in the casserole dish along with the stock, Worcestershire sauce, pearl barley and bay leaves. Cover and place in the centre of the oven and cook for approximately 2 hours until the meat is tender. Add some more hot stock if the sauce is too thick.
    Serve with crusty wholemeal bread.

## Eadle's Faggot Supper

**Ingredients**
8 fresh faggots
2 onions, skinned and chopped
2 tblsp fat *(ideally that left from a roasting joint)*
1 tblsp flour
275 ml / ½ pt good quality meat stock
salt and freshly ground pepper

**Method**
   Place the faggots in a pre-heated oven at 180° C or gas mark 4 for 15 - 20 minutes, until hot through. To make the gravy, gently fry the onions in the fat until soft. Blend in the flour, before gradually adding the stock to give a smooth gravy. Season to taste. Pour over the heated faggots and serve with creamy mashed potatoes and vegetables in season.

## The Beckley Breakfast

**Ingredients** *(Eadle's Farm Products)*
1 black pudding, sliced
1 white pudding, sliced
4 low fat pork sausages
4 rashers of dry cured green / smoked bacon

**Method**
   Fry, bake or grill the ingredients, beginning with the sausages. Serve with fried tomatoes and mushrooms.

## Fruit and Mushroom Stuffing

**Ingredients**
400 g / 1 lb fresh redcurrants
1 tblsp water
1 tblsp sugar
1 tblsp finely chopped onion
200 g / ½ lb chopped mushrooms
125 g / 5 oz minced pork / finely chopped streaky bacon
30 g / 1¼ oz butter
1 slice fresh bread, crumbed
1 clove of garlic, crushed
fresh herbs - 1 tblsp each chopped parsley and thyme
salt and freshly ground pepper
1 small egg to bind

**Method**
   Cook the redcurrants in the sugar and water until soft. Sauté the onions in the butter, together with the mushrooms, pork and bacon. Combine all the ingredients, except the egg, together and season to taste. Bind with the beaten egg. Use to stuff boned lamb or pork, prior to roasting.

# FISH

## Filleting Trout:
Fillets are readily available from Farmers' Markets, but for those wishing to do it themselves, follow a few simple steps:
1. Lay out the trout on kitchen paper to stop it slipping and, using a sharp knife, cut a vent along the belly as far as the tail.
2. Open out and press firmly along the backbone on the skin side, using your thumbs for pressure.
3. Turn the trout over and lift the entire bone easily away, using the sharp knife to loosen any side bones. Snip the end bone with kitchen scissors.

## Cooking Trout:
### Baking
Whole fish, steaks and fillets can be baked in a greased dish, or wrapped in individual foil parcels, in a moderately high oven for 20 - 30 minutes. There is no need to turn. Trout steaks take 8 - 10 minutes.
### Grilling
Slash the skin diagonally and brush both sides well with a bit of oil and lemon juice. Season and cook for approximately 5 minutes on each side. For fillets, lay skin side down on the grill pan rack for about 3 minutes, brushing again with the oil halfway through cooking.
### Pan Frying
Dust the fish lightly with seasoned flour and fry in hot oil, or a mixture of oil and butter for approximately 5 minutes each side, or 3 minutes for fillets.
### Microwave
Season with black pepper. Place on a suitable dish and cover and cook on full power for 2½ minutes in a 750 watt microwave oven. Allow to stand for 2 minutes before serving. For more than one fish allow extra time - refer to your manufacturer's cooking guidelines.

**Grading the trout at Brookleas Farm**

## Seared Trout Bruschetta with Horseradish

**Ingredients**
4 trout fillets
1 ciabatta or French stick, quartered
1 garlic clove, peeled
2 tblsp extra virgin olive oil
125 g / 5 oz crème fraîche
1 tblsp hot horseradish sauce
1 tblsp chopped chives
rocket or watercress to garnish
salt and freshly ground pepper
lemon juice and olive oil to serve

**Method**
To make the bruschetta, toast the bread under a grill or on a griddle, then rub all over with the garlic clove and drizzle with oil. Keep warm in a low oven. Combine the crème fraîche, horseradish, chives, salt and pepper.
Meanwhile lightly season the fillets and brush over a little extra oil. Heat a frying pan until really hot and sear the trout skin side down for 3 minutes, flip over and cook for a further 30 seconds..
Arrange the seared trout over the bruschetta with a dollop of the horseradish cream and some rocket leaves. Serve drizzled with lemon juice and olive oil.

## Trout in Honey

**Ingredients**
4 trout fillets
Marinade:
  2 onions, skinned and chopped
  2 tsp clear English honey
  1 tblsp oil
  4 mushrooms, chopped
  ½ glass of white wine
  1 tblsp chopped parsley
  1 tsp caraway seeds
  ½ tsp chilli sauce
  salt and freshly ground pepper

**Method**
Put the chopped onions and mushrooms in a long ovenproof dish and add the honey, wine, oil, caraway seeds, parsley, chilli sauce and seasoning. Put in the fish, cover and leave to marinate for ½ hour. Gently cook the fish in the marinade in a pre-heated oven at 180°C, or gas mark 4, for a further half an hour until cooked. Remove the fish and serve with a butter sauce.

## Tea Smoked Trout with Squash and Coriander Oil

**Ingredients**
1 kg / 2 lb *(approx)* butternut squash, peeled and cubed
6 tblsp extra virgin olive oil
½ tsp cayenne pepper
8 tblsp Jasmine tea leaves
8 tblsp soft brown sugar
8 tblsp long grain rice
600 g / 1½ lb chunky trout fillets
2 spring onions, chopped
1 tblsp chopped coriander
salt and freshly ground pepper
French beans to serve

**Method**
   Place the squash in a small roasting pan and stir in 2 tsp of hot oil, cayenne, salt and pepper. Roast it at 220°C or gas mark 7 for 15 - 20 minutes until golden and tender.
   Line a wok with a large sheet of foil allowing it to overhang on the edges. Mix together with the tea leaves, sugar and rice, spoon into the wok and place a trivet over the top. Cover it with a tight fitting lid and place on a high heat for 6 - 8 minutes until the mixture begins to smoke vigorously.
   Lightly season the trout fillets, quickly remove the lid and place the fillets, skin side down, on the trivet. Cover and cook for 5 minutes. Remove the wok from the heat, but leave it undisturbed for a further 3 minutes.
   Meanwhile, heat the remaining oil with the spring onion, coriander and a little salt for 3 minutes until softened, cool slightly and then purée in a spice grinder until smooth and vivid green. Divide the squash between plates, top with the trout fillets and serve with coriander oil and the French beans.

## Trout and Mushroom Bake

**Ingredients**
4 large trout fillets
1 small onion, chopped
25 g / 1oz butter
250 g / 10 oz mushrooms, chopped
100 g / 4 oz white breadcrumbs
25 g / 1oz parsley, chopped
salt and freshly ground pepper
juice of ½ lemon

**Method**
   Fry the onions in half the butter until golden. Mix with the mushrooms, breadcrumbs and parsley. Season to taste with freshly ground salt and pepper. Spread the mixture in an ovenproof dish. Lay the trout fillets on the top and dot with the remaining butter. Cover and bake at 180°C or gas mark 4 for 15 minutes. Uncover, sprinkle with the lemon juice and return to the oven for a further 5 minutes. Serve with new potatoes and a crisp green salad.

# PUDDINGS

Cross Lanes Fruit Farm

## Orange and Ginger Rhubarb Crumble

**Ingredients**
400 g / 1 lb rhubarb
1 large orange, grated rind and juice
½ tsp ground ginger
50 g / 2 oz demerara sugar
Topping:
   100 g / 4 oz self-raising flour
   50 g / 2 oz butter or margarine
   50 g / 2 oz caster sugar
   2 tblsp flaked almonds

**Method**
   Pre-heat the oven to 190°C or gas mark 5. Chop the rhubarb and place in a greased ovenproof dish together with the grated rind and juice of the orange, the ginger and the demerara sugar. Cook gently in the oven for 10 minutes.
   Rub the fat into the flour until the mixture resembles fine breadcrumbs. Stir in the sugar and sprinkle the mixture over the top of the fruit. Cover with the flaked almonds and bake for 25 minutes until golden brown. Serve with a dollop of creamy yoghurt.

## Gooseberry Soufflé

**Ingredients**
200 g / 8 oz gooseberries
50 g / 2 oz caster sugar
3 free-range eggs, separated
150 ml / ¼ pt double cream
1 packet of lime jelly
4 tblsp water
25 g / 1 oz ratafia biscuits, crushed

**Method**
   Dissolve the jelly in the water over a low heat. Make up to 275 ml / ½ pt with cold water. Meanwhile, cook the gooseberries gently for 10 - 15 minutes, stirring occasionally, until they are soft and broken up. Liquidise, pass through a nylon sieve, then measure 150 ml / ¼ pt of purée. Add this to the jelly, mixing well, then leave aside to begin setting. When it does begin to set add the egg yolks and whisk until the mixture is fluffy.
   Whip the cream until it is thick. Whisk the egg whites until they are very stiff. Gently fold both into the setting jelly until well blended. Turn the soufflé into a prepared 570 ml / 1 pt soufflé dish and chill in the refrigerator until set. Sprinkle with the crushed ratafia biscuits.

# Blueberry Pancakes

## Ingredients
Pancake:
   135 g / 5½ oz cornmeal *(polenta)*
   100 g / 4 oz self raising flour, sifted
   1 tsp bicarbonate of soda
   2 tblsp golden syrup
   50 g / 2 oz butter *(melted)*
   450 ml / 16 fl oz buttermilk or milk
   1 egg, beaten
   200 g / 8 oz blueberries
Raspberry Sauce:
   200 g / 8 oz raspberries
   2 tblsp golden syrup

## Method
   Place the dry ingredients in a bowl and mix together. Make a well in the centre and add the golden syrup, melted butter, milk and beaten egg. Mix to form a smooth batter. Stir in the blueberries. Drop 3 tblsp of the mixture on to a hot, lightly greased frying pan and cook for 2 - 3 minutes each side, until lightly browned. Remove from the pan and keep warm. Repeat until all the mixture is used up. To make the sauce, purée together the raspberries and the syrup and push through a sieve. Warm and serve on top of the pancakes.

# Floating Islands with Summer Fruit Sauce

## Ingredients
275 ml / ½ pt milk
2 drops of vanilla essence
135 g / 5½ oz caster sugar
4 free-range eggs, separated
Sauce:
   450 g / 1lb 2 oz raspberries, redcurrants and blackcurrants
   sugar to taste

## Method
   First make the sauce by simmering the fruits until they have produced juice, but not lost their shape. Sweeten it to taste and set to one side to cool.
   Simmer the milk, 35 g / 1½ oz sugar and the vanilla essence in a wide pan, but do not boil. Whisk the egg whites until they stand in firm peaks. Gradually whisk in *(1 tblsp at a time)* 25 g / 1 oz of the sugar until the meringue is stiff and glossy. Gently fold in a further 25 g / 1 oz of the caster sugar. Spoon out tablespoons of the meringue mixture and slide on to the heated sweetened milk. Cook for about 3 minutes *(do not overcook)*, turning once. Remove using a slotted spoon and drain on paper towels. Continue to poach until all the mixture has been used up. Strain the milk and reserve for the custard base.
   To make the custard, whisk the egg yolks with the remaining sugar. Pour the strained milk into the egg mixture, stirring continuously. Pour the custard mix into a heavy based saucepan and heat, still stirring, without boiling, until the mixture thickens. Cool, then pour into individual serving bowls. Arrange the poached meringues on top of the custard. Top with the cooled fruit sauce.

## Strawberry Amaretto Surprise

**Ingredients**
400 g / 1 lb strawberries, hulled
275 ml / ½ pt double cream
grated rind of 1 orange
2 egg whites
100 g / 4 oz caster sugar
3 tblsp Amaretto liqueur
150 g / 6 oz bag of marshmallows, chopped
75 g / 3 oz ratafia biscuits, crushed

**Method**
  Cut the strawberries in half, reserving 8 halves for decoration. Whip the cream until it is stiff, and mix in the orange rind. Whisk the egg whites until they form stiff peaks. Gradually incorporate the sugar and continue whisking. Fold the meringue into the whipped cream and add the Amaretto. Stir in the strawberries, marshmallows and crushed biscuits.
  Transfer to a serving bowl and decorate with the strawberry halves.

## Galliano Fondue

**Ingredients**
1 tin sweetened condensed milk
570 ml / 1pt double cream
Galliano liqueur to taste *(substitute another liqueur if preferred)*
200 g / 8 oz cream cheese
strawberries, or other soft fruit

**Method**
  Whip the cream until it is firm, then fold in all the other ingredients, apart from the soft fruit. Chill and serve with the fruit. This will freeze well, if you have any left over, to be used on another occasion.

## Marscarpone Raspberry Fool

**Ingredients**
400 g / 1 lb raspberries
200 g / 8 oz Marscarpone cheese
juice of ½ a lemon
1 - 2 tblsp caster sugar to taste
a little yoghurt

**Method**
  Reserve a few raspberries for the garnish. Purée the rest of the raspberries, then push the mixture through a nylon sieve. Mix the raspberry purée with the cheese. Add the lemon juice and sugar to taste. If the mixture is too thick, add a little yoghurt. If you want to add a little texture to the fruit fool, crush some Amaretti biscuits and stir these into the mixture.
  Spoon into long tall glasses and decorate with the whole raspberries.

***Fruity Tip!*** Picked too many strawberries? Purée them in a food processor, then pour into ice lolly moulds for the children (add a little icing sugar to sweeten). For adult palettes, freeze the purée until needed, then use as an ice cream topping with a little Vodka, Grand Marnier or other favourite liqueur!

## Raspberry Queen of Pudding

**Ingredients**
500 ml / 1 pt milk
100 g / 4 oz fresh white breadcrumbs
knob of butter
grated rind of a small lemon
200 g / 8 oz raspberries
2 free-range eggs, separated
50 g / 2 oz caster sugar
1 dstsp granulated sugar

**Method**
   Gently heat the butter and the milk until the butter melts. Remove from the heat and add the breadcrumbs and grated lemon rind. Leave to cool and then beat in the two egg yolks. Pour into a greased ovenproof dish and bake at 180°C or gas mark 4 for 30 minutes until set. Arrange the fruit on top. Whisk the egg whites until stiff, then add the caster sugar and continue whisking until the mixture stands in peaks. Spoon over the raspberries. Sprinkle the top of the meringue with granulated sugar, then return to the oven for 10 - 15 minutes until the meringue is golden. Serve warm with vanilla ice-cream.

## Raspberry Cheese Crunch
Serves 6

**Ingredients**
150 g / 6 oz Priory Oat biscuits ('Just Biscuits')
100 g / 4 oz melted butter
1 packet of rasberry jelly
1 thin skinned lemon
150 g / 6 oz full fat soft cream cheese
50 g / 2 oz caster sugar
250 g / 10 oz raspberries

**Method**
      Crush the biscuits and mix evenly with the melted butter. Spoon into 6 glasses.
      Beat the cheese with the sugar and the grated rind of the lemon. Place half the packet of jelly into a measuring jug and make up to 150 ml / ¼ pt with hot water. Stir it until it has dissolved and allow it to cool until it just begins to set. Beat it into the cheese a little at a time. When it is smooth, spoon over the biscuit base in the glasses and allow to set.
      Place the remaining half of the jelly into a measure and make up to 300 ml / ½ pt with hot water. Stir until it dissolves. Cool. When it is on the verge of setting, fold in the raspberries and carefully spoon over the mixture in the glasses. Chill until set.

# Eggy Bread

### Ingredients
4 slices of slightly stale bread
2 free-range eggs
a little milk
butter or oil for frying
lemon juice and sugar for serving

### Method
Beat together the eggs and the milk. Dip the slices of bread in the egg mixture and allow to soak up the liquid. Drain. Fry both sides until golden and serve with the lemon juice and sugar *(like traditional pancakes)*, or a summer fruit sauce. (see p 74)

# Plum Tart
*Serves 6*

### Ingredients
200 g / 8 oz shortcrust pastry
1 tblsp semolina
400 g / 1lb plums
50 g / 2 oz caster sugar
3 free-range egg yolks
1 tsp mixed spice
275 ml / ½ pt sour cream
50 g / 2 oz soft brown sugar

### Method
Roll out the pastry and line a 17.5cm / 7 in flan ring with it. Lightly prick the pastry to stop it rising during cooking. Sprinkle with semolina to stop the pastry becoming soggy.

Halve the plums, remove the stones and put the fruit to one side. Beat together the caster sugar, egg yolks, mixed spice and cream and pour into the flan. Arrange the plums on top and put in oven at 180°C or gas mark 4 and cook for 20 minutes. Then sprinkle the top with the brown sugar and the rest of the mixed spice and return to the oven for another 20 minutes.

# Honeyed Plums
*Useful for either fresh or frozen plums, which do not need thawing before use*

### Ingredients
3 plums per person
1tsp honey per plum

### Method
Lay the plums in the bottom of an ovenproof dish and cover with honey. Put in the bottom of cool oven, 120°C or gas mark ¼ and leave until plums soften. Eat hot or cold.

## Pear Upside Down Pudding
*It can be made more or less rich by putting more or less butter and sugar with the fruit*

**Ingredients**
25 g / 1oz butter
25 g / 1oz soft brown sugar
3 pears *(Conference or Glou Morceau - best when ripe but also works well if a little under ripe)*
Sponge:
   100 g / 4 oz butter
   100 g / 4 oz caster sugar
   2 free-range eggs
   150 g / 6 oz self-raising flour

**Method**
   Spread the bottom of an ovenproof dish with 1oz of butter and the soft brown sugar. Peel, core and halve the pears and place flat side down in the dish.
   Cream butter and sugar until pale and fluffy. Add the beaten eggs slowly while mixing. Fold in the flour and ginger *(if used)*. If necessary, add a little water to obtain a soft dropping consistency.
   Cover the fruit with this sponge mixture. Bake for 40 - 45 minutes at 160°C or gas mark 2½ until golden.
   Turn out onto a plate and serve with hot custard or whipped cream.

## Sage and Honey Poached Pears
*An unusual combination that both looks and tastes wonderful*

**Ingredients**
4 ripe pears
2 tblsp clear English honey
2 tblsp water
juice ½ lemon
2 sprigs sage
sage leaves for decoration

**Method**
   Peel the pears, keeping the stalks in. Trim the base and stand the pears in a saucepan. Mix the honey, water and lemon juice and pour over the pears. Add sprigs of sage. Bring to the boil and simmer until pears just soft, 10 - 20 minutes. Transfer to a serving dish or individual dishes, cool and decorate with new sage leaves.

## Auntie Phyllis' Apple and Almond Pudding

**Ingredients**
400 g / 1 lb cooking apples *(Bramley or Peasgood Nonsuch, which cook to a fluff)*
75 g / 3 oz butter
100 g / 4 oz caster sugar
50 g / 2 oz ground almonds
1 large free-range egg

**Method**
 Peel, core and chop the apples. Bring to the boil with 25 g / 1oz sugar and a minimum of water. Simmer until apples fluff, beat with a wooden spoon to make them smoother. Put them into a buttered pie dish and, if time, allow to cool.
 Cream the butter and remaining sugar. Stir in the ground almonds and egg. Spread mixture over the apples. Bake in a moderate oven 160°C or gas mark 2½, for about 40 minutes until golden.
 Serve with cream.

## Honey Apple Tart

**Ingredients**
300 g / 12 oz shortcrust pastry
1 kg / 2 lb *(approx)* cooking apples *(Bramley or Peasgood Nonsuch)*
5 tblsp clear English honey
grated rind and juice of a small lemon
25 g / 1 oz butter
1 tsp ground cinnamon
1 tsp apple brandy or Calvados
3 eating apples *(one each of Cox's Orange Pippin, Spartan, Russet)*

**Method**
 Peel, core and slice the cooking apples, then cook them in a little water until soft. Add 3 tblsp of the honey, the lemon rind, the butter and cinnamon and simmer uncovered until the mixture reduces to a thick purée. Allow to cool and stir in the brandy or Calvados.
 Line a 20 cm / 8 in flan ring with the pastry. Prick lightly with a fork to stop the pastry rising during cooking. Pour in the cooled apple purée. Core, but don't peel, the eating apples, halve and slice very thinly. Arrange on top of the purée and bake for 25 minutes at 200°C or gas mark 6. Place the remaining honey in a pan together with half the lemon juice. Heat until the honey dissolves and brush over the surface of the cooked tart to give it a shiny glaze. Serve with cream or custard.

PHOTO, CROSS LANES FRUIT FARM

# Honey Treacle Tart

### Ingredients
150 g / 6 oz shortcrust pastry
4 tblsp golden syrup
2 tblsp clear English honey
1 tblsp lemon juice
50 g / 2 oz fresh white breadcrumbs

### Method
Using threequarters of the pastry, line a 17½ cm / 7 in pie plate. Prick lightly with a fork to stop the pastry rising during cooking and crimp the edges. Add the lemon juice to the syrup and the honey. Mix in the breadcrumbs. Spread the filling on to the pastry base.

Roll out the remaining pastry into strips and make a lattice pattern across the tart. Bake at 200°C or gas mark 6 for 30 minutes.

Serve with honey sweetened custard.

*Recipe reproduced by kind permission of Ruth Mead, Honey Cookery, Northern Bee Books*

# Black Forest Roulade
Serves 8

### Ingredients
125 g / 5 oz caster sugar
6 large free-range eggs, separated
50 g / 2 oz cocoa powder
Filling:
   220 ml / 8 fl oz double cream
   1 jar of 'Home Farm' black cherry conserve
   dash of Kirsch *(optional)*
icing sugar for dusting

### Method
Prepare a 30 cm x 17.5 cm / 11½ in x 7 in Swiss roll tin by lining it with lightly oiled greaseproof paper. Pre-heat the oven to 180°C or gas mark 4.

Put the egg yolks in a basin and whisk until they start to thicken. Add the caster sugar and continue to whisk until the mixture thickens slightly, taking care not to over whisk. Carefully mix in the cocoa powder. In a separate bowl, whisk the egg whites until they reach the 'soft peak' stage. Carefully blend the egg whites into the chocolate mixture. Pour into the tin and level out. Bake for 25 minutes on the middle shelf of the pre-heated oven.

Remove from the oven and allow to cool in the tin *(it will shrink during this process)*. When completely cold turn out on to a fresh sheet of greaseproof paper dusted in icing sugar. Remove the piece of greaseproof paper used for cooking.

Spread the black cherry conserve, mixed with Kirsch, over the cake. Whip the cream and spread over the black cherry conserve. Gently roll up the cake like a Swiss roll - it is normal for it to crack a little - removing the paper as you go. Dust the finished cake with a little more icing sugar.

# CAKES

# Carrot Cake

### Ingredients
200 g / 8 oz wholemeal flour
1½ tsp baking powder
2 tsp cinnamon
100 g / 4 oz butter
100 g / 4 oz demerara sugar
100 g / 4 oz clear English honey
200 g / 8 oz carrots, grated
25 g / 1 oz chopped nuts
lemon juice
Topping:
   25 g / 1 oz butter
   100 g / 4 oz icing sugar
   50 g / 2 oz soft cream cheese
   3 drops vanilla essence

Sift the flour, baking powder and cinnamon into a large bowl. In a saucepan melt the 100 g / 4 oz butter, sugar and honey until they are smooth and runny. Pour into the bowl of flour and add the carrots, nuts and a little lemon juice. Mix together thoroughly. Put into a greased loaf tin and bake at 180°C or gas mark 4 for 45 minutes until golden. Remove from tin and allow to cool.

Make the topping by mixing together the butter, icing sugar, cream cheese and vanilla essence to form a smooth paste. Cover the top of the cold cake.

# Honey Cherry Cake

### Ingredients
200 g / 8 oz self-raising flour
100 g / 4 oz butter
3 free-range eggs
pinch of salt
100 g / 4 oz caster sugar
2 tblsp clear English honey
50 g / 2 oz glacé cherries, chopped
milk to mix
Topping:
   25 g / 1 oz flaked almonds , toasted
   25 g / 1 oz glacé cherries, quartered
   2 level tblsp clear English honey

### Method
Pre-heat the oven to 180°C or gas mark 4. Cream the butter and the sugar until light and fluffy. Beat the eggs well with the 2 tblsp honey and mix with the sugar and the butter. Stir in the cherries. Sift the flour and the salt and carefully fold into the cake mixture. Add a little milk if it appears too dry.

Put into a greased cake tin and bake for about 1 hour *(check after 45 minutes)*. Turn out and cool on a wire rack. Heat the honey for the topping until warm, add the almonds and the cherries and spoon over the loaf.

## Apple Cake
*This is a gooey cake that keeps well. Use a cooking apple that fluffs up such as Bramley or Peasgood Nonsuch if you want a smooth texture or a variety that holds its shape such as Fiesta or Egremont Russet if you want separate apple pieces.*

### Ingredients
400 g / 1 lb apples, peeled, cored and cut into chunks
300 g / 12 oz plain flour
1½ tsp bicarbonate of soda
¼ tsp salt
150 g / 6oz butter
150 g / 6oz caster sugar
150 g / 6oz raisins
50 g / 2 oz chopped walnuts
150 ml / ¼ pint milk
2 tblsp brown sugar for top

### Method
Grease and line a 20 cm / 8 in square tin.

Gently cook the apples in a minimum of water until they fluff, then beat until smooth or until just soft to retain pieces. Sieve the flour, bicarbonate of soda and salt and rub in the butter. Add the rest of the ingredients except the brown sugar and mix well. Put the mixture into the tin and spread evenly. Sprinkle brown sugar over the top.

Bake in oven at 160°C for 1½ hours or until 'springy'. Cool for 5 minutes, then turn out and finish cooling on a wire tray. Store in an airtight tin.

## Lord Lieutenant's Cake

### Ingredients
150 g / 6 oz self-raising flour
50 g / 2 oz ground almonds
300 g / 12 oz mixed dried fruit
100 g / 4 oz butter
100 g / 4 oz caster sugar
1 free-range egg, beaten
125 ml / 4 fl oz Lord Lieutenant's Ale
         (Chiltern Brewery)

### Method
Simmer the fruit, butter, sugar and ale together in a fairly large pan for about 20 minutes and allow to cool. Add the egg, ground almonds and self-raising flour and mix well.

Turn into a greased 17.5 cm / 7 in cake tin and bake for 2½ hours at 140°C or gas mark 1.

# Bruce Bogtrotter's Cake

## Ingredients
200 g / 8 oz good quality plain chocolate
150 g / 6 oz unsalted butter
200 g / 8 oz caster sugar
4 tblsp plain flour
6 free-range eggs, separated
Topping:
   150 g / 8 oz plain chocolate
   220 ml / 8 fl oz double cream

## Method
   Melt the 200 g / 8 oz of chocolate and the butter over a low heat *(or use a microwave oven)*. Add the flour, sugar and lightly beaten egg yolks. Whisk the egg whites until stiff. Gently fold half the beaten egg whites into the chocolate mixture, mixing thoroughly. Fold in the rest.
   Spoon the cake into a 20 cm / 8 in round tin and bake at 180°C or gas mark 4 for 40 minutes. If tested, the cake will appear to be underdone, but it will firm up as it cools.
   For the topping, melt the chocolate in a bowl with the cream, then spread over the cooled cake.

# "All-in-one" Sponge

## Ingredients
100 g / 4oz self-raising flour
1 tsp baking powder
100 g / 4 oz butter or soft margarine
100 g / 4 oz caster sugar
2 large free-range eggs
2 - 3 drops vanilla essence
'Home Farm' strawberry jam
icing sugar for dusting

## Method
   Lightly oil and line with greaseproof paper, two 18 cm / 7 in round cake tins. Pre-heat the oven to 170°C or gas mark 3.
   Sift the flour and baking powder into a large bowl. Add all the other ingredients except the jam and the icing sugar. Whisk until thoroughly combined. Divide the mixture between the two tins and bake in the centre of the oven for about 30 minutes.
   When cooked, remove from the oven and leave for thirty seconds. Loosen the edges with a palette knife and turn the cakes out on to a wire cooling rack. Peel off the greaseproof paper and leave to cool. Spread the 'Home Farm' strawberry jam over one of the cake halves, and place the other half on the top. Dust the cake with icing sugar.

# MISCELLANY

## Summer Fruits Jam
*Makes 1.2 kg / 3 lb jam, based on 650 watt microwave oven*

**Ingredients**
200 g / 8 oz hulled strawberries
100 g / 4 oz raspberries
300 g / 12 oz 'topped and tailed' blackcurrants
1 kg / 2lb 3 oz preserving sugar
knob of butter
75 ml / 3 fl oz brandy

**Method**
   Place the strawberries *(cut up large strawberries)*, raspberries and blackcurrants in a non-metallic oven proof bowl. Microwave on HIGH setting for 7 minutes. Mash gently and stir in the butter and sugar. Microwave again on HIGH for 14 - 16 minutes, stirring halfway through the cooking time. The mixture should boil vigorously for 4 minutes during this time. Test the jam to assess its setting properties. Stir in the brandy; pot and cover.

## Tomato Relish

**Ingredients**
600 g / 1½ lb tomatoes, chopped
200 g / 8 oz cucumber, peeled and chopped
25 g / 1 oz salt
2 garlic cloves, skinned and chopped
1 red pepper, deseeded and chopped
275 ml / ½ pt spiced vinegar
50 g / 2 oz demerara sugar
½ tsp mustard powder

**Method**
     Place the tomatoes and cucumber in a bowl and sprinkle with salt. Cover and leave overnight, then drain and rinse before placing in a large pan. Add the garlic and the red pepper. Blend the remaining ingredients together, stir into the vegetables and bring the whole lot slowly to the boil. Turn down the heat and leave to simmer for about 1 hour until the mixture is soft. Pot into sterilised jars and cover in the usual way. Leave to mature for several months.

## Sloe Gin Chutney
*After making your sloe gin keep the gin soaked sloes to make a delicious chutney*

**Ingredients**
400 g / 1 lb sloes, previously soaked in gin
200 g / 8 oz onion, skinned and finely chopped
200 g / 8 oz cooking apple, peeled, cored and finely chopped
200 g / 8 oz raisins
570 ml / 1 pt vinegar
200 g / 8 oz dark brown muscavado sugar
1 tsp ground cloves
1 tsp ground cinnamon

**Method**
    Cook the sloes in the vinegar for 15 minutes to soften them, then allow them to cool. Remove the stones *(best to dive in with your hands!)*. Add all the other ingredients, heat until the mixture bubbles, then simmer until the chutney is thick - up to an hour. Remove any stones that may have been missed earlier.
    Whilst waiting for the chutney to cook, prepare the screw top jars. First wash them thoroughly in hot soapy water, rinse and then dry them off in a the oven. Pour the thickened chutney into these hot, dry jars, filling to the top. Seal with undamaged, clean screw top lids, ensuring a tight fit. When the jars cool the lid will be depressed, indicating an airtight seal.

## Mulled Cider

**Ingredients**
1 large bottle of cider
2.5 cm / 1 in stick of cinnamon
pinch of nutmeg
pinch of allspice
3 whole cloves
¼ cup of clear English honey

**Method**
Combine the cider, spices and honey, heat slowly and simmer for 15 minutes. Strain and serve hot with a slice of orange or lemon.
*Recipe reproduced by kind permission of Ruth Mead, Honey Cookery, Northern Bee Books*

## Celebration Summer Punch

**Ingredients**
1 bottle of 'Skippetts', medium or medium dry white wine *(Boze Down Vineyard)*
1 litre *(just under 2 pints)* of lemonade
1 lemon
1 cucumber
borage or lemon leaves

**Method**
    Wash and cut the lemon into quarters lengthwise. remove the central core and pips, then slice very thinly. Cut the cucumber in half lengthwise, or if small, leave whole. Slice up very thinly.
Pour the wine and lemonade into a punch bowl, then add the lemon and cucumber. Stir. Chill well before serving.
Decorate with a few sprigs of borage or some lemon leaves.
*For a drier punch use tonic water instead of lemonade.
For a sweeter punch use a bottle of Boze Down 'Ambrozia' wine and lemonade.*

# Ready-made Produce at the Farmers' Market

As well as the stallholders at the markets being able to provide raw ingredients for recipes, some prepare ready to eat goods for sale. So if you can't be bothered to make your own, the WI stall is perhaps the best place to head. Tempting home made cakes - fruit cakes, sponge cakes, chocolate cakes, tarts, flans and pies are just a few examples of items snapped up at every market. They also do a wide range of jams and chutneys. 'Home Farm' also make jams, jellies, chutneys and mincemeat, as well as a range of delicious home-made cakes. Ivy Newman specialises in jams, jellies, marmalades and a variety of curds.

If it is biscuits you want, 'Just Biscuits' may have what you are after. They offer seven varieties of sweet shortbread or oat based biscuits and five savoury. Special presentation packs are available throughout the year.

If you are seduced by the smell of freshly baked bread, then stop off at Vincent Charles' stall - the pile of organic loaves soon vanishes.

'Eadles' cook on site, if you are tempted by a sausage in a roll or a bacon buttie. They also sell cold cooked meats, and other prepared foods, such as pork pies.

Both trout and mushroom stallholders offer extras such as soups, pâtes and marinated produce.

If it's drink you are looking for to accompany your meal, or just to enjoy, then several stalls offer a variety of fresh organic fruit juices. Alcoholic tipples range from original beers to fine English wines.

# MENUS

Health eating is about achieving a balanced diet, with plenty of variety. Eat plenty of fruit and vegetables and fresh food, low in fat and rich in starch and fibre. Above all, food is to be enjoyed

The following menus are suggestions using recipes from the book.. Substitute as necessary to suit

## Breakfast

Organic Fruit Juice

The Beckley Breakfast (p66)
Fried Tomatoes
Fried Mushrooms

Bread and Home-made Jam
or Marmalade

Tea or Coffee

## Brunch

Spinach, Leek and Cheese wtih Pasta (p29)

Crusty Bread

Apple Cake (p83) or Fresh Fruit

Tea or Coffee

## Ploughman's Lunch

Potato and Leek Soup (p 23)

Bread and Cheese

Cold Meats

Carrot Cake (p 82) or Fresh Fruit

Chiltern Brewery Ale

## Children's Specials 1

Special Toad-in-the-Hole (p63)
Baked Sliced Potatoes (p 33)
Vegetables in Season

Honeyed Plums (p 77)
Vanilla Ice Cream

Apple Juice


## Children's Specials 2

Spiced Highland Meatballs (p 54)
Marais Salad (p 38)

Raspberry Queen of Pudding (p 76)
Vanilla Ice Cream

Organic Fruit Juice


## Children's Specials 3

Beefburger Whopper (p 54)
Sliced Tomatoes

Raspberry Cheese Crunch (p76)

Ginger Beer

## Summer Picnic

Devilled Eggs (p 26)

Smokey Crispy Bacon Salad (p 40)

Bread

Plum Tart (p 77) or Fresh Fruit

English Wine

## Summer Barbeque

Berkshire Barbeque Lamb Steaks (p 57)
or
Barbeque Sausages with Apple and Orange Sauce (p63)

Tomato and Basil Salad (p 39)

Bread

Blueberry Pancakes (p74)

Celebration Summer Punch (p 87)

## Bonfire Supper

Thick Autumn Soup (p 25)

Eadle's Faggot Supper (p 66)

Honey Treacle Tart (80)

Mulled Cider (p 87)

## Summer Dinner Party

Surprise Pears (p 27)

Trout in Honey (p 69)

Highland Escalopes with Fresh Tomatoes,
Black Olives and Basil (p52)
New Potatoes
Garden Peas

Foating Islands with Summer Fruit Sauce (p 74)

Cheese and Biscuits

Coffee

## Winter Dinner Party

Carrot and Orange Soup (p 24)

Tofu and Coriander Cakes (p30)

Chinese Crispy Duck with Plum Sauce (p 48)
Wilja Parsnip and Onion Roast (p 32)
Steamed Green Vegetables
Mashed Potatoes

Honey Apple Tart (p79)

Cheese and Biscuits

Coffee

Dinner Party Recipes can be accompanied by
English wines from the Boze Down Vineyard

# Index

Apples:
   Apple Cake 83
   Apple Vichyssoise 23
   Auntie Phyllis' Apple and Almond Pudding 79
   Barbeque Sausages with Apple
      and Orange Sauce 63
   Cross Lanes Chicken 43
   Honey Apple Tart 79
   Sausages in Cider 62
Bacon:
   Gammon Cooked in Ale, and Caramellised
      in Mash Tun Marmalade 64
   Redman's Bacon and Pineapple Stir-fry 64
   Smokey Crispy Bacon Salad 40
Beef:
   Adrienne's Beef and Mushroom Casserole 53
   Beefburger Whopper 54
   Casserole of Highland Beef with Prunes
      and Pickled Walnuts 52
   Highland Beef Pilaff 53
   Highland Brisket with Creamy Mustard and
      Caramellised Shallot Sauce 50
   Highland Escalopes with Fresh Tomatoes,
      Black Olives and Basil 52
   Pot-roast Topside of Highland Beef with
      Root Vegetables 51
   Spiced Highland Meatballs 54
Breakfast, The Beckley 66
Broad Bean Special 34
Cakes:
   "All-in-one" Sponge 84
   Apple Cake 83
   Bruce Bogtrotter's Cake 84
   Carrot Cake 82
   Honey Cherry Cake 82
   Lord Lieutenant's Cake 83
Carrot:
   Carrot and Butternut Squash Soup 24
   Carrot Cake 82
   Carrot and Orange Soup 24
Cheese:
   Carrot Cake 82
   Celeriac and Potato Crunchy Mash 31
   Celery with Cheese Filling 27
   Cheesy Pork Steaks 60
   Fried Mozzarella 27
   Galliano Fondue 75
   Marais Salad 38
   Marscapone Raspberry Fool 75
   Obelix Cheese and Potato Jackets 33
   Pasta and Cheese Salad 40
   Pork and Mushroom Casserole 61
   Raspberry Cheese Crunch 76
   Ravioli with Ricotta Filling 28
   Spinach, Leek and Cheese with Pasta 29
   Surprise Pears 27
   Tomatoes with Parmesan and Ricotta Filling 28
   Vegetable Parcels 30

Chicken:
   Anila's Chicken Tikka 42
   Chicken and Mushroom Casserole 43
   Chicken Supreme with Watercress Sauce 42
   Cross Lanes Chicken 43
Chinese Crispy Duck with Plum Sauce 48
Chutney, Sloe Gin 86
Cider, Mulled 87
Dressing, Honey 36
Duck:
   Chinese Crispy Duck with Plum Sauce 48
Eggs:
   "All-in-one" Sponge 84
   Black Forest Roulade 80
   Blueberry Pancakes 74
   Bruce Bogtrotter's Cake 84
   Curried Eggs 26
   Devilled Eggs 26
   Eggy Bread 77
   Floating Islands with Summer Fruit Sauce 74
   Gooseberry Soufflé 73
   Honey Cherry Cake 82
   Marais Salad 38
   Mayonnaise 36
   Potato and Egg Salad with Avocado Dressing 38
   Raspberry Queen of Pudding 76
   Special Toad-in-the-Hole 63
Faggot Supper, Eadle's 66
Game:
   Blackcurrant Venison Steaks 47
   Bodger's Game Pie 46
   Jugged Hare 45
   Poacher's Pot 44
   Pot Roast Venison 47
   Venison Casserole 48

Honey:
  Honey Apple Tart  79
  Honey Cherry Cake  82
  Honey Dressing  36
  Honey Treacle Tart  80
  Honeyed Plums  77
  Roasted Parsnips with
    Honey and Mustard Glaze  32
  Sage and Honey Poached Pears  78
  Trout in Honey  69
Jam, Summer Fruits  86
Lamb:
  Berkshire Barbeque Lamb Steaks  57
  Colin's Lamb Casserole  55
  Country Lamb Stew  56
  Foxbury Noisettes  57
  Minced Lamb Curry  56
  Spring into Summer Stew  56
Mayonnaise  36
Mushrooms:
  Adrienne's Beef and Mushroom Casserole  53
  Chicken and Mushroom Casserole  43
  Cream of Mushroom Soup  22
  Ostrich Fillet Steaks with Mushroom Sauce  65
  Pork and Mushrooms  60
  Stuffed Mushrooms  26
  Trout and Mushroom Bake  70
  Trout and Mushroom Salad  39
  Vegetable Parcels  30
Ostrich:
  Ostrich Fillet Steaks with Mushroom Sauce  65
  Ostrich Hotpot  65
Parsnips:
  Roasted Parsnips with Honey and Mustard  32
  Wilja Parsnip and Onion Roast  32
Pears:
  Pear Upside Down Pudding  78
  Sage and Honey Poached Pears  78
  Surprise Pears  27
Pork:
  Barbeque Sausages with Apple and
    Orange Sauce  63
  Carribean Pork Jerk  58
  Cheesy Pork Steaks  60
  Fruity Pork Curry  59
  Pork and Macaroni Casserole  61
  Pork Escalopes with
    Stir-fry Red Cabbage and Prunes  60
  Pork Mince Stir-fry  61
  Pork and Mushrooms  60
  Pork Wellington  59
  Sausages in Cider  62
  Special Toad-in-the-Hole  63
Potatoes:
  Baked Sliced Potatoes  33
  Celeriac and Potato Crunchy Mash  31
  King Edward's Champ  32
  Mash Stir-fry  31
  Obelix Cheese and Bacon Jackets  33
  Potato and Egg Salad with Avocado Dressing  38

  Potato and Leek Soup  23
  Potato Samosas  34
Puddings:
  Auntie Phyllis' Apple and Almond Pudding  79
  Black Forest Roulade  80
  Blueberry Pancakes  74
  Eggy Bread  77
  Floating Islands with Summer Fruit Sauce  74
  Galliano Fondue  75
  Gooseberry Soufflé  73
  Honey Apple Tart  79
  Honey Treacle Tart  80
  Honeyed Plums  77
  Marscapone Raspberry Fool  75
  Orange and Ginger Rhubarb Crumble  73
  Pear Upside Down Pudding  78
  Plum Tart  77
  Raspberry Cheese Crunch  76
  Raspberry Queen of Pudding  76
  Sage and Honey Poached Pears  78
  Strawberry Amaretto Surprise  75
Punch, Celebration Summer  87
Rabbit Casserole  44
Relish, Tomato  86
Salads:
  Italian Salad  37
  Marais Salad  38
  Pasta and Cheese Salad  40
  Potato Salad with Avocado Dressing  38
  Rocket and Strawberry Salad  39
  Smokey Crispy Bacon Salad  40
  Tomato and Basil Salad  39
  Trout and Mushroom Salad  39
  Winter Vegetable Salad  37
Snacks / Starters:
  Celery with Cheese Filling  27
  Fried Mozzarella  27
  Ravioli with Ricotta Filling  28
  Spinach, Leek and Cheese with Pasta  29
  Stuffed Mushrooms  26
  Surprise Pears  27
  Tofu and Coriander Cakes  30
  Tomatoes with Parmesan and Ricotta Filling  28
  Vegetable Parcels  30
Soups:
  Apple Vichyssoise  23
  Carrot and Butternut Squash Soup  24
  Carrot and Orange Soup  24
  Cream of Mushroom Soup  22
  Pea and Ham Soup with Croûtons  22
  Potato and Leek Soup  23
  Thick Autumn Soup  25
Stuffing, Fruit and Mushroom  66
Trout:
  Seared Trout Bruschetta with Horseradish  69
  Tea Smoked Trout with Squash and
    Coriander Oil  70
  Trout and Mushroom Bake  70
  Trout and Mushroom Salad  39
  Trout in Honey  69

## Acknowledgements:

Thanks is given to all those stallholders who contributed recipes related to their own products *(Details about the various traders is given on pages 9 - 18)*. Where these recipes have been obtained from an outside source an acknowledgement is given beneath the recipe. Himley Farm near Bicester, Tel: (01869) 343349, no longer attends the market, but has provided some of the pork recipes.

Particular thanks is given to Mark Hillyer, the Market Co-ordinator, for his support and work, and Gill Franklin of Cross Lanes Fruit Farm, who helped with the proof-reading.

Where photographs have been supplied an acknowledgement is given beside the image. Other photos have been taken by Clive Ormonde of MAP READING

Thanks is given to those who support the market generally - RISC (see p 7), Reading Borough Council, The Thames Valley Farmers' Association.

Thanks to computer technology for making the publication of this book possible.

Part of the funding for this project has been provided by 'Awards for All' lottery grant.

Margaret Ormonde, MAP READING